Finding Silence

Finding Silence

52 Meditations for Daily Living

James Roose-Evans

First published 2009

The History Press
The Mill, Brimscombe Port
Stroud, Gloucestershire, GL5 2QG
www.thehistorypress.co.uk

British Library Cataloguing in Publication Data.
A catalogue record for this book is available from the British Library.

ISBN 978 0 7524 5405 4

Typesetting and origination by The History Press
Printed in Great Britain

For Celia Read who initiated the London Meditation Group, and to its members, as well as all those other groups who meet to share in the silence beyond the silence

In meditation go deep into the heart

Lao Tzu

Life is so good, despite everything, when you are awake in the depths
of the heart

Abhishiktananda

Contents

Foreword
by Mark Tully

In one of his meditations James quotes the motto of the Dominicans, the intellectual order of the Roman Catholic Church. Translated from Latin the motto is 'to contemplate and to pass on to others the fruit of our contemplation.' That is just what James has done in *Finding Silence*. Each of us who reads these meditations will find fruit which is particularly nourishing for us, because the tree which bears the fruit is James' experience. These are not impersonal, or theoretical meditations. 'Meditations for Daily Living', they are grounded in his experience of life.

James has found that meditation can still the busy mind, which he compares to chattering monkeys leaping from tree to tree. It is also a way to the centre in each of us, a centre in which we can be given answers to the questions which disturb us fundamentally, often without us realising it. They are the questions about our identity: Who am I? Where have I come from? Where am I going? The centre is also a refuge from the blows that descend on our fragile egos. James knows all about those blows because he has worked all his life in the theatre, a precarious, insecure profession, full of rivalry and jealousy.

My career of forty years in journalism, a profession which also often involves more than its fair share of blows to the ego, has been a roller-coaster of highs and lows, inflations and deflations. I have tried to see the inflations and the deflations, particularly the inflations, as dangerous imposters, to use Kipling's word, but I still find myself sometimes nursing a bruised ego, or suffering a hangover from a high. I suffer from the fear of failure, which seems to me to come from the fear of a blow to the ego – better even not to try than to risk is the way I sometimes find myself thinking. In this way, I found the meditation 'Death Was Like a Game I Could Not Win' particularly relevant to my life. In this meditation James describes the fear of failure which drove the renowned rugby international Jonny Wilkinson. He didn't know how to free himself from it, and because his play was so obsessive he never knew what it meant to be really happy. After a series of injuries Jonny Wilkinson came to Buddhism and meditation where he found his fulfilment was no longer about 'self-gratification', but about 'seeing the happiness of others.' He came to believe that his fear of failure had arisen out of an even deeper fear of death, an inability to answer one of the questions that James has found can be answered in the centre to which meditation leads us. Jonny Wilkinson's fulfilment in seeing the happiness of others leads me on to James' insistence that meditation is not intended to produce the feel-good factor, nor is it intended to be a form of self-analysis. As the Dalai Lama says, 'meditation and the pursuit of wisdom should always issue forth in acts of compassion for others.' That means that we should listen to others as well as 'listening inwardly.'

James says, 'life's real journey is towards the kind of person each of us is meant to be.' He speaks of Jung's belief that each child comes into the world with a blueprint for life. In the meditation 'A Tree Being Motionless Birds Come To It' we see that through contact with our inner resources 'we gradually discover that our life has been going somewhere, however blind we have been to its direction, and however unhelpful to it we ourselves have been.' Coming to understand our own personal blueprint, reading the signposts which point to the next stage in our lives, recognising the blockages which tell us we have taken a wrong turning, are all essential if we are to avoid trying to become or to remain the person we are meant to be. As James puts it, 'We have to learn how to co-operate with time and destiny, allowing life to shape us rather than trying to shape it to our own ends.' This surely is the opposite of how our modern individualistic, competitive, culture, tells us we should live.

Herein lies an apparent contradiction. The idea of each of us having a blueprint for life emphasises our individuality. James even discusses the possibility that we might each have our own angel. At the same time meditation has given him an acute awareness of his being part of something infinitely greater than himself. In the meditation 'Look At The Stars! Look, Look Up at the Skies!' he writes, 'meditation sharpens the sight and the insight and deepens our sense of wonder, whether we believe in God or not. Believers and unbelievers alike can contemplate the mystery of the universe with awe and humility.' Looking up at the stars at night in remote parts of India where the sky is clear and not polluted by artificial light I have sometimes been overcome with a feeling of being an infinitely small part of something immeasurably large, yet mattering, for all that. Being a Christian I believe that to be an experience of God.

James is an Anglican priest yet he does not set out to convert the reader. He believes, 'it is in the silence of meditation that we begin to transcend our differences of opinion, culture, dogma, and personality.' He acknowledges that even differences between those who believe in God and those who don't can be transcended, and points out that even atheists report having spiritual experiences. Most unfortunately, as I see it, there are those, and they are not small in number, who have opened a gap between spirituality and religion. James' book is intended to be a bridge over that gap. It is a bridge because it's written by an avowedly religious man yet someone who any reader will recognise as deeply spiritual too. For him each religion is 'a sign pointing in its own way to the divine mystery.'

The divine mystery can not be defined in terms that would satisfy a scientist, or indeed a lawyer, but it can be portrayed in music, in art, and in poetry. Nature displays it, too, and James' meditations bring home to me, above everything else, an awareness of our oneness with nature and hence our oneness with the universe. James is an artist, a highly respected theatre director, and someone who has read deeply, so he has illustrated his meditations with an abundance of quotations from poetry and literature, but perhaps my favourite quotation is one that he has written himself: 'One has only to sit quietly in a garden in spring, in the early hours, and become aware of invisible lines criss-crossing the garden as birds flit and whirr about their tasks, never colliding. We too are birds of passage and yet we are part of the whole. We move through time and yet eternity is all about us. We are all a part of the eternal pattern and rhythm of the universe.'

Introduction

Spiritual life is a response to a call … Someone calls to us from within the depths of the heart, awakening our deepest longing. This call is like a golden thread guiding us deeper and deeper within, always pointing to the beyond.

> Llewellyn Vaughan-Lee in *Catching the Thread:*
> *Sufism, Dreamwork and Jungian Psychology*

Walking across Westminster Bridge at the end of a very demanding rehearsal, I said to my assistant, 'Where do you get your calm from?' He replied, 'I meditate for an hour each morning.'

'Where did you learn to meditate?'

'I went to live in an ashram in India for six months and learned the breath meditation.'

He then turned to me with a smile.

'Where do you get your calm from?'

And I replied, 'I also meditate.'

There will be those who, reading this, will ask how a man of theatre comes to be writing a book on meditation. After all, theatre is one of the toughest and most ego-centric of professions. What the public does not see are the long periods of unemployment when no work comes or, if it does, is unsuitable. The theatre is an over-crowded profession full of insecurities.

Actors, directors, designers, writers, rise and fall with alarming rapidity, often for no discernible reason. As the actress Claire Bloom wrote in her autobiography: 'The life of an actor is peppered with blows to the ego'. For those of us who work in show business it is an itinerant and uncertain life and in order to survive we have to find a centre within ourselves. That centre, quite obviously, cannot always be our work. And this is increasingly true of everyone for, as automation takes over so many jobs and redundancy always looms on the horizon, the changing pattern of society is forcing us all to find an identity that lies deeper. Yet if we can measure up to the challenge there is an unique opportunity here for growth both as individuals and as a society. The changing social and economic patterns are forcing us to find new answers to the questions: Who am I? Where have I come from? Where am I going?

The 1960s saw the rise of a great meditation movement which has continued to gather momentum to this day. Zen and Yoga are no longer seen as a monopoly of the East but have become part of world culture while Transcendental Meditation (TM) which was introduced to the West by the Maharishi Mahesh Yogi is now practised by tens of thousands in the West. The practice of meditation has even penetrated the upper echelons of the business world and is part of the training programme of such worldwide organisations as the Royal Dutch/Shell Group. Among Christians the first dialogue between them and Buddhists was initiated by the Quakers, while individuals such as the Cistercian Thomas Merton, the Jesuit William Johnson, the Benedictine Pere Déchanet (whose book *Christian Yoga*, was written some fifty years ago), all sought to integrate the teachings of Buddhism, Zen, or Yoga with their Christian beliefs. More recently, in 2005, the BBC's TV series *The Monastery*, which featured five very modern men living the monastic life at Worth Abbey in England for forty days and nights, attracted an audience of three million viewers. In the month following the programme, the Abbey's website received 40,000 visits and during the same period hundreds of people signed up to go on retreat at the Abbey. Abbot Christopher Jamison observes in his subsequent book on the series, *Finding Sanctuary* that those who came on retreat were individuals with no background of religious faith. 'They are a new generation of people who have not lapsed from faith but for whom religion is a closed book '.

What is less known, however, is the long tradition of meditation in both Islam and Judaism. The Jewish visionary tradition, known as the Kabbalah, goes back several hundred years and resulted in the movement known as Hasidism. This tradition taught that the only way in which we can unite the warring opposites in the human psyche is by the practice of meditation. The Kabbalah used a wide variety of techniques, believing that it is more important for individuals to find the one that best suits their needs. The aim, as also in the Eastern notion of one-pointedness, is to be as completely focused as possible in the present moment by concentrating on whatever image, sound, or mantra their particular method advocates. The chief goal of the Jewish mystical tradition is to bring the divine into ordinary life. Thus, during the founding of Israel, the Chief Rabbi of Palestine, Abraham Isaac Kook, until his death in 1935, constantly preached about the need to integrate the physical, emotional and spiritual aspects of ourselves. 'The old way of choosing one path' he also wrote, 'and following it patiently can no longer prevail. We have developed far beyond this. To embrace all paths and to integrate them into a full and secure harmony, this is the beginning of our sacred responsibility.' Similarly Father Bede Griffiths, in his ashram in Southern India, would hold up a hand and pointing to each finger in turn, say, 'This represents Hinduism, this Judaism, this Islam, this Buddhism, this Christianity, but here...' pointing to the centre of his palm, ' here at the centre is where we all meet.' Constantly, in his later years, he would urge people 'Go beyond!' and Ed Hussein in his book *The Islamist* says,

'Rumi taught me that the religion of Love transcends all other religions; for lovers, the only religion and belief is God.' The Qur'an accepts religious diversity, creedal plurality. As the Prophet says, 'To you your religion, and to me mine.'

Such are the times we live in that we can no longer focus on trying to convert people to our particular religion – or even our way of meditation. Rather we need to listen to one another's stories and in this way learn from each other. Only in this way will our spirituality be enriched and grow. As the great mystical book of Judaism, *The Zohar* teaches: There is a vast unseen web that links each of us. We are all individual buds on the great Tree of Life. In countless ways everything we think, say and do is regarded as having an influence on the whole. As Joseph Jaworski observes in his book, *Synchronicity: The Inner Path of Leadership*, published in 1998, 'All human beings are a part of that unbroken whole which is continually unfolding from the Implicate and making itself manifest in our Explicate world.'

Although as a child I was without any religious background – as a family we never went to church – nonetheless, from an early age, I have always been conscious of another and deeper dimension to life which led me first, on my own initiative, to be confirmed as an Anglican, then later to be received into the Roman Catholic Church, and all this was deepened by years of Jungian analysis. Eventually I ceased practising as a Catholic and whenever I had to fill in a form requiring me to state my religion I would write the word 'Seeker'. You might have thought that that would have aroused the curiosity of any hospital chaplain but never did one come near me! Then, in the late 1950s, a School of Meditation was set up in London. I enrolled and was given a mantra to repeat mentally. The process was complicated, however, by the fact that each week the voluntary counsellors kept changing and each seemed to give contradictory advice. In the end I stopped going and persevered on my own.

This search for a deeper spiritual centre was happening to me at one of the most demanding periods of my life. Only someone who has started an enterprise from scratch, without any financial backing, can understand the unremitting slog of running a shoestring organisation. The Hampstead Theatre, which I founded in 1959, began from nothing, lurching from one financial crisis to another. At that time there was no fringe theatre in London and it was to be seven lean years before we began to receive help from the Arts Council of Great Britain.

In 1973 I resigned as Artistic Director in order to develop a freelance career as a director and writer. Then in 1989, while teaching workshops in America, I was given a slim volume of letters entitled *84 Charing Cross Road* by Helene Hanff. I acquired the stage rights, adapted it and in 1981 directed the world première at the Salisbury Playhouse from where it transferred to the West End for eighteen months, while in 1982 I went to direct it on Broadway with an American cast. But in the summer of 1981, while the many events of this outer journey were unfolding, another, and inner, journey was nearing its completion when in Hereford Cathedral I was ordained as a priest of the Anglican Church. Two weeks later I was in Salisbury, starting rehearsals for *84 Charing Cross Road*.

It had been some four years earlier that a priest friend said to me one evening, 'James, why don't you take Holy Orders?' I thought deeply about this but at the same time I was clear that I was not meant to give up my work in the theatre. Later, however, I learned about the non-stipendiary ministry, the members of which include farmers, doctors, teachers, financiers – I was to be the first theatre director – each of whom earns his living like most people but each of whom exercises a particular ministry but who also often knows what it is to be unemployed, declared redundant, or be self employed, like countless others. Then in the 1970s I began writing a weekly article on meditation for *The Church Times* which led eventually to my first book on meditation, *Inner Journey: Outer Journey*. It was a book aimed at those Christians who have moved beyond rote Christianity that basically emphasises 'morality' issues, and who feel drawn to meditation as a way of finding a spiritual centre to their lives. It was also intended for those seekers after truth who often find it difficult to relate to existing forms of Christianity. As a senior cardinal at the Synod of Bishops of the Catholic Church observed in Rome, November 1985, 'People are searching for the sacred in their lives – but outside the Church.' Many today, while sympathetic to the Church and the ancient truths that it teaches and represents, nevertheless find that many of these truths are being taught more effectively outside the institutional churches. There is a gap widening between religion and spirituality, and there is an urgent need for bridges to be built. It was to provide one such bridge that I wrote the book. As a priest I have not had to exercise conventional parish duties and it was always recognised that my ministry would be unorthodox. It has, in the main, been concerned with reaching out to those outside the Church, and meeting them where they are. 'Our real journey in life,' wrote Thomas Merton, 'is interior. It is a matter of growth, deepening, and an even greater surrender to the creative action of love and grace in our hearts. Never was it more necessary for us to respond to that action.'

One of the chief attractions of the practice of meditation for so many is that it is a natural technique, not dependent upon any theology or dogmas. One of the most vivid illustrations of the benefits of meditation is that of a fifteen-year-old schoolboy, quoted in a recent book, *Teaching Meditation to Children*, by David Fontana and Ingrid Stack. Prem comes from Thailand where he was taught from an early age to meditate by his parents, long before coming to Britain. He is popular with his classmates not only for his calm and cheerful nature, but for his unassuming success at sport and academic work. He says that he cannot imagine being without meditation, that it would be like living in only one part of himself. Yet meditation does not cut him off from the world. 'Meditation teaches that nothing outside can touch the real me. It puts me more in touch with things; but allows me to see them for what they are, without sort of being sucked in all the time.' What meditation does is to reconnect us with the inner core of our being.

Both in Britain and America, as also in Ireland, more and more people are coming together to meditate. The initiative is usually taken by one person who invites others to join. As one woman, who had started such a group, wrote to me, 'Numbers have gone up and there are now seventeen names on the list. The newest member is a Muslim, and is a most courageous stick of dynamite, even facing disapproval from her mosque for, basically being a female who's prepared to rock the boats! It just touches me that there is this deep need for silence. Afterwards we stay on and talk over a cup of tea. The keen response to this opportunity for quiet communion has touched me deeply – it is clearly so vitally needed.' As Thomas Merton said at a gathering in Calcutta of abbots of Catholic monasteries and representatives of Asiatic religions, when he asked everyone to join hands and form a circle, 'We are going to have to create a new language of prayer, and this new language has to come out of something which transcends all our traditions, and comes out of the immediacy of love.'

The pages that follow have grown out of talks that I have given informally to a small group that meets regularly in London, which was initiated by a friend who is a psychotherapist and painter. I did not seek to lead such a group but, like so much in my life, it simply happened and I have gone with it. The group is composed of eight psychotherapists, one GP, one artist, one publisher, one theatre agent, one teacher of the Alexander Technique, and two counsellors. Most of these I would describe as agnostics, although one is a committed Buddhist, and one has been a Sufi. Each, however, is aware of the need for a spiritual direction in their lives, of a need to find a way of centring down that will give deeper meaning to their lives and work.

There is no obligation to attend regularly but although each is a busy professional some make a long journey to be present, often over an hour. Again this is not an uncommon feature in such meditation groups. We do not ask if members meditate regularly, nor what form of meditation they practise, though in the main most observe the breath meditation. We make no demands. Each of us, however, realises that we are making an individual journey and yet, at the same time, gain support from meeting regularly. Perhaps part of the attraction of such small groups lies in the recovery of a sense of community which by and large our society today has lost. What we have found is that not only is the silence very powerful within the group but that the sharing of individual reflections afterwards often reaches a great depth of insight. We learn from one another and grow through the shared experience.

People begin to arrive on the first Sunday of each month at around quarter past five and assemble in the front room to chat, exchange news, or perhaps welcome a newcomer to the group. After about half an hour a bell is rung and everyone goes into the back room where a circle of chairs has been arranged, with a low table in the centre on which there may be a lit candle, a bowl of water, or a vase of flowers. The telephone is unplugged and after a short talk a Tibetan gong is sounded and there follows a half hour of meditation the end of which is signalled by the gong. Everyone takes their own time in coming out of the silence which is rather like rising to the surface after being on the bed of the ocean.

Wine or fruit juice is then offered and occasionally some simple refreshment. I believe strongly in the simple ritual of 'breaking the bread', inspired by the example of Pope John Paul II, when he was Bishop of Cracow, who would invite people to his apartment, believers and non-believers, to share wine and a simple *oplatek*, a round wafer. This simple ritual recalls for me the words of John Keats from a letter to a friend in which he speaks of 'the wine of love and the bread of friendship'. During the conversation that follows, still seated in the circle, one person may ask to share a dream, another may want to develop something said in the introductory talk, or it may be a question about the practice of meditation itself.

Assembling in one space at the beginning and then moving into another for the meditation is very much part of Quaker practice. A Quaker Meeting takes place at eleven o'clock on a Sunday morning and those arriving assemble first in an outer room to chat, before slowly moving into the Meeting Room, so that by eleven o'clock everyone is assembled and the silence has already commenced. In all religions one finds such a *temenos*, a sacred space, separated from the outside world.

I recall being invited to a Buddhist meditation in a private house in the woods in northern Michigan. From the moment of arrival we were conscious of crossing a threshold as we were quietly greeted by our hostess and invited to remove our shoes before entering the room set aside for the meditation. This inner room was lit only by candlelight. At one end was a statue of the Buddha to which, as in all halls of meditation, we bowed, not in worship but acknowledging the Buddha within each one of us. A gong announced the beginning and end of the meditation. As we departed we bowed again to the image of the Buddha, and to the space itself, before quietly departing. Such a simple ritual of obeisances, of shedding one's footgear, of speaking quietly, of silence, helps to emphasise that one is crossing over into a sacred space: 'the ground on which thou walkest is holy ground.'

It is in the silence of meditation that we begin to transcend our differences of opinion, culture, dogma, and personality. It is in this silence that we begin to have a glimpse of the unity of all things and of all creation. The American actor Jake Gyllenhaal, star of *Brokeback Mountain* and *Rendition*, who is a practising Buddhist, recently remarked, 'My life occupies all the spaces between my performances and that's where it's really at!' It is when we let go of all our preoccupations and busyness and allow ourselves to be in the spaces in between that we begin to experience what Eckhart Tolle calls 'The Power of Now', or Eliot 'between two waves of the sea'. Such an awareness did the author Dennis Potter have shortly before his death when, in a televised interview with Melvyn Bragg, he said, 'The only thing you know for sure is the present tense. I can celebrate the now-ness of everything. If people could only see that! There's no way of telling you. You have to experience it for yourself. Below my window in Ross the blossom is out in full. It is the whitest, frothiest, blossomest blossom that there could ever be. I *see* it!'

But if the growing interest today is upon spirituality rather than upon religion, what exactly do we mean by the spiritual? For many it suggests crystals, tarot cards and much else, but that is not it. The word itself occurs with increasing frequency nowadays in the media as in this example from *The Sunday Times* for 6 January 2002:

> There is a spiritual crisis all over the Western world. People hunger for a framework of meaning and purpose that can transcend the individualism and selfishness of the competitive market. They want to be connected to some higher vision of good and find some way for their lives to contribute to that good.

By spirituality, therefore, we mean that dimension which gives our lives meaning and calls us towards a higher self, usually expressed in some form of relationship with a Divine Being, but not always. Even atheists report having spiritual experiences, epiphanies, and an awareness of the 'is-ness' of everything. There are thousands of websites on the internet under such headings as 'Atheist spirituality' and even one 'Atheists for Jesus'. Some atheists would say that spiritual things are a very important dimension of life to them and that music, which Joyce Grenfell regarded as the greatest of all arts, 'the closest to Spirit', opens the door to that dimension. And the same may be said of all true art. A door opens upon an awareness of continuity, of timelessness, and of a fundamental belief in goodness and love. It is as though we glimpse at such moments another pattern as Wordsworth observes in his *Ode on Intimations of Immortality*:

Hence in a season of calm weather
Though inland far we be,
Our souls have sight of that immortal sea
Which brought us hither;
Can in a moment travel thither,
And see the children sport upon the shore,
And hear the mighty waters rolling evermore.

The spiritual would appear to be part of our make-up as human beings, and so our spiritual journey is one with the emotional and psychological. This is why the psycho-therapeutic or analytic process has an important part to play in clearing the ground for the growth of the spiritual, for until we can view objectively our often irrational behaviour it is difficult for the spiritual to grow. It is like a garden: until the ground is cleared of weeds, bright shoots of everlastingness cannot break through. How can we grow in compassion if our emotions are frozen or we continually project our *shadow* side onto others? A recurring image in dreams is often that of a house in which unsuspected rooms are discovered, or dry rot is found, or the dreamer descends to a dark and murky cellar. In dreams, as also in reality, we may have many locked rooms within us which have never been opened, and no light penetrates through to them. It is not surprising that we speak of skeletons in cupboards. Until we have learned to open up all our inner rooms and let light into them we cannot expect to grow spiritually.

It is here, perhaps, that we need to distinguish religion from spirituality. Religion is a structure invented by human beings to enable them to give expression to their spiritual yearnings and to nurture the spiritual dimension of their lives. Religion provides a framework with a belief system, a moral code, an authority structure, and a form of worship within which people can find both nourishment and community. But what often happens is that such structures become fossilised and our energies are no longer vitalised by them. The latter half of the twentieth century saw hundreds of thousands leaving the particular form of Christianity into which they had been born, and exploring further afield to find their own means of spiritual growth because the beliefs proposed so authoritatively no longer seemed to ring true. Such beliefs were often at variance with people's experience in that their spiritual needs were not being nourished by what the Churches, in the main, had to offer. It is not following a religion but, as the Sufi master Inayat Khan once wrote, 'it is *living* a religion which is necessary.' No religion is complete in itself. Each is a sign pointing in its own way towards the Divine Mystery. Every major religion has similar ideas of love, has the same goal of benefitting humanity through spiritual practice. Each religion has some aspect of truth to contribute to all the others as Father Bede Griffiths, Abhishiktananda, and many others have constantly emphasised.

David Hay, who for more than twenty-five years has been engaged in empirical research into the nature of religious or spiritual experience, is convinced that spiritual awareness is biologically built into the human psyche and that this holistic awareness of reality is found potentially in every human being 'whatever their religious beliefs or none.'

Although historically spirituality has very close links with religion it is logically prior to religion. Religious understanding can grow out of the recognition by individuals of the existence of such spiritual experience within themselves. It was Sir Alastair Hardy, the zoologist, who in 1966 first offered a naturalistic account of religious experience when he suggested that religious awareness is a biological phenomenon that has evolved in the human species through the process of natural selection because it has survival value. If we accept his hypothesis then religious experience cannot be limited to members of any particular religion or, indeed, to religious people in general. Everybody, including those who have no religious beliefs, must be, at least potentially, in possession of such awareness. There is, it would seem, such a thing as secular spirituality.

Spirituality has to do with the inner depths of the individual. It is only when we listen inwardly and attentively to the claims of the spirit that renewal comes. As the Oracle at Delphos proclaimed: 'O Man, look well within thyself and thou shalt find therein a well of Truth for ever springing up!' In listening, however, to the claims of the spirit within, many have to learn first how to discard much unnecessary baggage, such as those images of God on which they were brought up or which have been inherited through their culture. A child learning the alphabet will have a book which begins with a picture of an apple and the words: A is for Apple, followed on the next page by a picture of a bird and the words: B is for Bird, until he reaches: G is for God. And so throughout the ages people have fashioned many images of God in an attempt to understand that which is beyond our finite comprehension. If as children the image of God as a loving avuncular figure helps us, fine; but we have to be prepared to move on, shedding images as we go until, hopefully, one day we do not need any images at all and, like Meister Eckhart, are able to acknowledge that 'God is no thing.' I remember one woman on the radio, expressing her anger with God, saying that when her sister had cancer she prayed to God, saying that if He saved her sister's life, she would devote her life to Him, but that God did not listen because her sister still died. When people get angry with God it is really with themselves that they are angry, although they don't see this. It is not God but their image of Him, their projection of God, with which they are angry. If we believe that God is some kind of whizz-kid at a vast bank of computers, trying to deal with billions of requests, then inevitably at some point we are going to be disillusioned and angry when He doesn't reply to our e-mails! Similarly it is no good praying for a fine day for the church outing when the farmer is praying for rain! Too often, even very intelligent people just don't use their intelligence where God is concerned. For centuries when people lost something they would pray to St Anthony to find it for them and attribute their success in finding it to his intervention, instead of realising that this is simply a mental note to one's subconscious, like knocking your head on the pillow five times if you want to wake up at five o'clock. Part of the problem, of course, is that the available language about God has been allowed to become too narrow, too anthropomorphic, and no longer functions as a satisfactory vehicle through which people can articulate their highest life aims.

'A man's God,' suggests Don Cupitt, the Sea of Faith theologian, 'is that which he worships, that which has over-riding authority in his life, that which matters most to him, that which most profoundly determines his sense of himself and the aim of his life, that which expresses the deepest truth of what he is. "Show me your God," runs an old saying, "and you show me what you are."'

I

'No time to say, Hello! Goodbye!'

The major problem, however, for so many today, is that so many of us are in danger of becoming like the White Rabbit in the film version of *Alice*, 'I'm late! I'm late for a very important date! No time to say, Hello! Goodbye!'

We are all rushing places, caught up in a whirl of activity, afraid to stand still for a moment, with no time to stand and stare and, most of all, afraid of silence, so we surround ourselves with musak, mobiles, the television, anything that will drown out that still small voice, until one day we wake up to find that time has run out like sand in an hourglass. It is then that, like Shakespeare's Richard II, we realise, 'I wasted Time, and now Time wastes me.' Suddenly with a shock, we realise our time is up.

However, before we reach such a realisation that 'irretrievable Time is flying' as Virgil expresses it, there are moments when we are conscious that behind all the frenzied activity we have an important date to keep here and now. At such moments we sense that behind this present reality there is another dimension of reality when, as Wordsworth puts it, 'our souls have sight of that immortal sea which brought us hither.' And yet, and yet, we continue to put off the task, saying 'I can deal with that later. There is plenty of time.'

It is because we do not take time that, repeatedly, we fail to heed the wisdom that is in our bodies, in our dreams, in our intuitions. But once we do begin to listen to this inner wisdom, then we begin to realise that 'there is a time and a season for everything under the sun.' Once we begin to understand that our lives wax and wane like the seasons, that for each of us there is a springtime as well as a time for harvest and a time for winter, a time for living and a time for dying, the better we shall understand the whirligigs of Time and be less threatened by life's vicissitudes.

There is a time and a season for everything and we have to learn how to trust Time and to accept that we are not masters of our destiny. When I was at the Crypt Grammar School in Gloucester we had to sing the following words every term from a poem by W.E. Henley, a former pupil: 'I am the master of my fate. I am the captain of my soul.' It is not so! As we grow older we begin to perceive that it is not we who are shaping our lives but, rather, that life is shaping us. Indeed, as we sail the seas of Time in our fragile coracles we begin to glimpse that our real journey is towards the kind of person each of us is meant to be. Jung believed that each child comes into the world with a blueprint for life and that the task for each one of us is to realise that blueprint as fully as possible. As Joyce Grenfell once said in a Dialogue at St Mary le Bow in London, 'I am less and less interested in being Joyce Grenfell, the performer, and more and more in becoming the person God meant me to be.'

The passage from Ecclesiastes appears to be full of contradictions. For instance we are told to speak and yet are also counselled to be silent; to love and yet to hate; that there is a time for peace and a time for war; a time to embrace and a time not to embrace. The key to all these seeming paradoxes is Time itself. It is knowing when is the time to do one thing and not another. I recall one demanding period in my life when I used to consult that ancient book of wisdom, the *I Ching*. I was always full of ideas and acted on impulse. But at this period the answer would unvaryingly be: Your idea is a good one but now is not the time! We have to learn how to co-operate with time and destiny, allowing life to shape us rather than trying to shape life to our own ends. As the Tao teaches: Wisdom is to be found by living in harmony with the flow of things rather than trying to control events. And so the question arises: how are we best able to go with the flow? There is no one route, but a variety of ways, and each of us has to choose the one that is best for us, and so it becomes a matter of experimenting until we find our own path. For some it may be through the practice of Tai Chi, as so many found under that great teacher Gerda Geddes, or through Yoga, or by way of meditation. The practice of meditation is thousands of years old and simply requires, as we read of Jesus, that we go apart into a lonely place and pray. Whether we meditate well or ill is not the point. There are no diplomas in the art of meditation. It is enough simply to meditate. As a Zen saying puts it: A journey of a thousand miles begins on one's own doorstep! One makes a path by walking!

Learning to Meditate

Though there are various techniques of meditation there is one prime requisite and that is a proper posture. The true relation of body, mind and spirit is something which we – especially the pew-oriented Christians of the West – are still slow to understand. In Japan, however, it lies at the centre of the ancient teaching of Hara (the Japanese word for the Vital Centre in each of us), while in India the practice of Yoga, and in China that of Tai Chi, have pursued a similar path. Japanese who practise Hara rest upright and composed, their whole being gathered inward. Such a person cannot be thrown off-balance – as in the many illustrations of the Boddhi-dharma who brought Zen Buddhism to China and whose image is still given to children in the form of a tumbler doll with a round lead-weighted belly which always brings him back to his upright position no matter how often he is knocked down.

Those who practise Hara have a right balance with themselves and others, with animals and even objects. I recall a story told to me once by my Jungian analyst, Dr Franz Elkisch who, as a Catholic, had many clients who were monks, nuns or priests. One of his clients was a nun who was very restless in herself and the despair of her community. Nothing that she did ever came right; she was at sixes and sevens with herself and others, always breaking things and having accidents. She was Sister Twenty-Two Misfortunes! In her analysis Dr Elkisch discovered she had been brought up in India and he loaned her a book by the Benedictine monk Pere Déchanet, *Christian Yoga*. As she began to practise Yoga in her cell, so she began to rediscover the relationship between her body, mind and spirit. No one in the community knew about this apart from her Abbess. Then one day the community's sewing machine broke down and no one was able to repair it. Suddenly this nun 'knew' that she could put it together. The others all laughed saying she would only make things worse. She persisted however and succeeded in repairing the machine. From then onwards, instead of things coming apart in her hands, they came together and the community began to see her in a new light. Her whole relationship with herself and with the community had changed.

Our physical posture reveals our inward posture. Only when the body is at ease is the mind at ease. The two go hand in hand. Seated, with both feet firmly planted, the knees slightly apart, and the hands resting on the knees, one sits with closed eyes and erect spine. If you slump, says one master, 'you will lose yourself. You will not be in your body'. And then one begins to meditate. The exercise of sitting, wrote Karl Durkheim, is the most fundamental of all. A thousand secrets are hidden in simply sitting still. 'A person who has once learned to collect himself completely in his sitting will never again let a day pass without practising for at least half an hour, for it is this which gives complete inner renewal, especially when one has learned to concentrate exclusively on the sitting, emptied of all thoughts and images.'

While there are a variety of forms of meditation, especially in Buddhism, basically there are two forms of meditation: one is observing the breath as it comes in and as it goes out, while the other involves mentally repeating a mantra, which is a sacred word or phrase. In India it is usually one of the sacred names of God such as *Ram*, while in the Christian Meditation Movement founded by the English Benedictine monk, Dom John Main, it is *Maranatha*, a Sanskrit word meaning 'Come, Lord!' For those who are approaching meditation for the first time the practice of following the breath is perhaps the simplest. The aim of both techniques is to still the busy chattering mind and rest in the silence. We breathe in, we pause momentarily, and then we allow the breath to be released, and rest in that 'space between two breaths', until the breath of its own accord begins again to fill up our lungs. Distractions will arise, thoughts of this and that, past resentments, unresolved problems, erotic fantasies even, for the mind is like a chattering monkey, leaping from branch to branch, doing its utmost to distract us. Patiently we acknowledge each distraction and return to concentrating on the breathing. Breathing in and breathing out. If we follow a mono-theistic religion then it can help to imagine that one is breathing God in and then breathing God out to the world. Many find it helpful, especially at the start, to count the breaths up to seven: breathing in and breathing out counting as one breath, and so on. If our mind wanders and we lose count we simply go back to the beginning and start all over again. It is a little like training a young puppy. We say to our busy mind: Sit! Be still! The counting acts merely as a traffic warden to ensure we don't get in the wrong lane. At the start the breaths may be long and deep but later they may become shorter and shallower, almost imperceptible. It is less a matter of controlling the breath than of allowing the breath its own length. The pause after having breathed in, and the pause after having breathed out, is like the gap between two waves of the sea. Over time our awareness of that gap at each end will become more important than the breathing in and breathing out; indeed, that gap, that space, that stillness, is what Eckhart Tolle means by 'the Power of Now'. The real world, says one Buddhist teacher, 'is beyond our thoughts and ideas. We see it through the net of our desires, divided into pleasure and pain, right and wrong, inner and outer. To see the universe as it is, you must step beyond the net. It is not hard to do, for the net is full of holes.' After a time we may find ourselves using a mantra but this will be dealt in the pages that follow. We remember again the Zen saying : A journey of a thousand miles begins on one's own doorstep!

But before we engage in meditation, as Buddhism teaches us, we should first begin by thinking, 'I am doing this practice not solely for my own benefit but also for the benefit of all sentient beings.' There is nothing narcissistic about true meditation as our practice reaches out to include all others and, as in the words of Jesus, 'For their sakes I sanctify myself.' It is important to stress this as often people look on meditation as simply a form of self-help or feel-good therapy. It is much more than this. And when our meditation comes to an end we should not rush into the next thing, thinking, 'I've done that! Now what's next?' but take time to come out of the silence, before moving gradually into whatever we have to do next. In this way we carry with us that quality of awareness, of mindfulness, that we have been experiencing during our meditation.

3

The Secret Garden

Sometimes on a summer's evening, with the windows open, I can hear the voices of children playing in the garden and then I am reminded of the important role played by the children in Frances Hodgson Burnett's classic *The Secret Garden*. In the story, on one of his rare visits, Mr Craven, Mary's guardian, asks her if there is anything she wants.

'Might I,' quavered Mary, 'might I have a bit of earth?'

'Earth? What do you mean?'

'To plant seeds in – to make things grow – to see them come alive,' falters Mary.

'Do you care about gardens so much?' said Mr Craven slowly. 'A bit of earth?' he repeated. 'You can have as much earth as you want. When you see a bit of earth you want take it, child, and make it come alive.'

Which is what Mary does. Aided by Dickon and the old gardener, she discovers the rusty key that opens the door of the secret garden which the young Mrs Craven was starting to create just before she died when giving birth to Colin, Mr Craven's sickly, bed-ridden son. Towards the end of the book Mr Craven who is in Switzerland – ten years on and he is still grieving for his young wife – has both a dream and a letter urging him to return to Yorkshire. As he approaches the secret garden, which to his knowledge has been closed and neglected ever since his wife's death, he hears the laughter of children. The next moment they all come racing out: Mary, Dickon, and Colin, his son, no longer an invalid but a healthy boy. Mr Craven says to him, 'Take me into the garden, boy, and tell me all about it.' As he looks around in amazement at what the children have done he says, 'I thought it would be dead.' And Colin replies, 'Mary thought so at first. But it came alive.'

It is when we nurture the seeds of meditation in our own inner garden that we, too, begin to come alive at a deeper level than that of mere happiness. Happiness is elusive: it comes and goes. What grows and becomes evergreen in our innermost garden is contentment. What the book is also saying is that Nature is often our best teacher. All who garden know how much one learns from tending the earth and plants. Mirabel Osler in her book, *In the Eye of the Garden* writes, 'Gardeners have to believe that the dead will reincarnate. It is not only the plants that bloom with such perverse bravado in the midst of winter that I love but also the dead black sticks of winter. Pick one and know with absolute certainty at that moment you are holding summer.'

The world is indeed '... charg'd with the grandeur of God.' as Manley Hopkins wrote. One has only to sit quietly in a garden in spring, in the early hours, and become aware of the intricate trajectory of invisible lines criss-crossing the garden as birds flit and whirr about their tasks, never colliding. We, too, are birds of passage and yet we are part of the whole. We move through time and yet eternity is all about us. We are all a part of the eternal pattern and rhythm of the universe. Therefore we should honour all creation. There is indeed a deep wisdom in nature. The secret life of trees is itself a subject for meditation. Each year we see enacted the pattern of our own lives, from the first waxen leaves of the chestnut, to the rich canopy of summer. Then comes the glory of autumn when the trees in their maturity blaze with new colours before letting fall their raiment to stand naked to the wind and the rain and the snows. With what recklessness the wind strips the trees bare, hurling and hurtling clouds of leaves like swarms of bees. Then it is that we see the tree in all its essential beauty of form, acquiring, as we should in age, a new beauty. And yet the tree is still growing though it seems dead, for from deep below the ground the sap is rising and new growth is at work. Often, gazing at the winter trees I am reminded of George Herbert's line: 'In age bud again'.

St Bernard of Clairvaux wrote in one of his letters: 'What I know of the divine sciences and of Scripture I learnt in the woods and fields. I have had no other masters than the beeches and the oaks. You will learn more in the woods than in books. Trees and stones will teach you more than you can acquire from the mouth of a teacher.' Elizabeth Barrett Browning also wrote:

Earth's crammed with heaven,
And every common bush afire with God;
But only he who sees takes off his shoes.
The rest sit round and pluck blackberries.

It is only when we begin to look, not only outwardly but inwardly, that we begin to experience everything as vital and living, and discover the truth of Blake's phrase: 'Everything that lives is holy.' We discern the great within the small, the extraordinary within the ordinary, a world in a grain of sand and eternity in a flower.

The entire cosmos is one burning bush. As Élémire Zolla has written:

The ideal forms of minerals, plants, animals, shape the single members of the species. Every rose seed contains the dream, the incorporeal image of a full-blown rose. The day one starts sensing the invisible dreams urging rocks, seeds, bodies and minds all around us on their predestined course, the first step towards wisdom has been taken.

This awareness of a holistic relationship with Nature is central to the very nature of spirituality. It requires us to go beyond ego-centricity and to take account of our relatedness to other people, to the environment. It is, above all, a matter of rediscovering a child's sense of wonder: to make things grow, to see them come alive.

 4

Basking in God

A certain brother went to his Abbot and asked him for some words of spiritual comfort. The Abbot said to the monk, 'Go and sit in your cell. Your cell will teach you everything.' We read of Jesus that he rose early and went up into a high mountain, into the wilderness, into a lonely place, in order to pray. He went apart and prayed. And if possible the place where we meditate should always be the same space, for such a space used regularly for prayer or meditation gathers to itself its own concentration of energy. In India, even in a crowded room there is usually a corner with a curtain drawn across where each member of the family goes in turn to meditate. It does not shut out the noise but it does become a sacred space, a place apart. Noise is a problem from which we cannot altogether escape. Our jangled nerves may well cry out for quiet so that even the ticking of a clock may cause us to wrap it in a scarf and put it inside a drawer. Sometimes it can help to remove the immediate source of irritation in this way, but we can also all too easily become neurotic about noise when, in fact, the noise is inside us. If we can just continue sitting still and accept the ticking of the clock, it will gradually merge into the background. Even if we do remove one source of noise there will always be others: a jet overhead, the squeal of brakes or revving of a car outside, the voices of people next door, the blare of someone's radio or television. I was once at a BBC conference to do with religious broadcasting when we were led in a guided meditation by a so-called expert on meditation who refused to start until a transistor radio playing somewhere outside the building had been located and turned off. In the meantime we sat there waiting until this was accomplished. Ironically the song that was being played was the famous Beatles song, 'Let it be! Mother Mary, pray for me,' which would have provided an ideal starting point for the meditation! Gradually we learn to let things be as we allow ourselves to be drawn into a deeper silence so that all these noises come to be heard at a distance and, in time, scarcely at all. If we are interrupted in our meditation, we should not be like the man who, as his wife enters the room to look for something, snaps, 'Can't you see I'm trying to meditate? For Christ's sake, it's difficult enough without you barging in and out all the time!' If we are interrupted in our meditation, if, for example, someone passes through the room, we should accept that interruption, even smile or make a comment, and then return to our meditation.

'Day after day,' says the Bhagavad Gita, 'let the Yogi practise the harmony of the soul in a secret place, in deep solitude, with upright body, head and neck, which rest still and do not move; with inner gaze which is not restless but rests still between the eyebrows. Then his soul is like a lamp whose light is steady, for it burns in a shelter where no winds come.'

In Wales I have a chair in my bedroom, facing a window that looks out onto fields, hills, woods and, in the distance, the Clee Hill which, when the peak is covered in snow in the winter, looks like Mount Fuji. Sometimes after heavy rain the whole countryside seems rinsed, translucent with colours. And in winter, when there is deep snow, and a full moon, the bare trees cast their shadows like X-rays across the blue-tinted snow. Occasionally a shy fallow deer appears or, very early in the morning, a hare makes its way across the lane. Sheep graze on the far field and the woods are full of pheasants, greater-spotted woodpeckers, a pair of ravens, foxes and badgers and other wildlife. On the windowsill stands a small icon of Our Lady of the Threshold, from Mount Athos, and on either side of it, in china candlesticks, are two tall candles, while in front of it, its pages open, is a book of the sayings of Lao Tzu. Even by day the flames of the candles are reflected in the glass of the window but even more so at night – as though there were another dimension beyond the one I am seated in.

A friend recently sent me a card of the Upper Basilica of St Clement in Rome, saying 'James, I lit a candle and said a prayer here for you.' Similarly another friend did the same thing for me at the shrine of St Melangell in Pennand Melangell in the Berwyn mountains. Lighting a candle is as much an act of poetry as it is an act of piety. Electric candles can never be the same! A wax candle, by contrast, is seen to diminish even as its flame stretches upwards. It is as though in the very act of giving light it diminishes itself ('to give and not to count the cost') while the flame is vulnerable to draughts and can be easily extinguished. Unlike an electric candle it is a vibrantly living presence so that when we leave the church, or temple, we know that even as it dies down and goes out, it will be replaced by other candles and other flames just as other prayers will be added to ours. All over the world people are coming and going in holy places and shrines, lighting candles and votive lamps, and saying prayers, reminding us of the story of Pentecost when tongues of fire descended on those present, reminding us also how people long to be set on fire, to be inspired, as in these words from the Book of Esdras: 'I shall light a candle of understanding in thy heart which shall not be put out.' An old craftsman in Spain, observing the late Polish poet, and translator of Pope John Paul II's poems, Jerzy Peterkiewicz, lighting a candle in front of an icon at his house, said, 'You are not doing that for Him, for He is surrounded by light, but to remind yourself that this tiny flame is in you.'

'God can be known to us in the same way as a man can see an endless ocean by standing on the shore at night with a dimly lit candle,' writes St Symeon the New Theologian. 'Do you think he can see much? Not much, almost nothing. Yet, nevertheless, he sees the water well. He knows there is an ocean in front of him, that this ocean is huge, and that he cannot see it all at once. The same is true of our knowledge of God.' And so I sit at my window, the candles reflected in the panes of glass, and the night sky beyond, and I recall the words of Una Kroll who, when asked how she prayed, replied, 'I sit at my window and bask in God.'

In a Dark Wood

A garden that has been carefully weeded can suddenly, after heavy rains, or just neglect, sprout fresh weeds. Similarly on a clear day in summer, literally out of the blue, an electric storm can erupt. So, too, even in the closest human relationships, misunderstandings can spring up like weeds, violence can erupt like a storm, occasioned by some unexpected turn of events or by something said or done by one or the other. At such times, where once there had been deep closeness, it can seem as though the two people are miles apart. Even after many years of friendship such emotion can be so violent that one or both are tempted to terminate the relationship, as accusations and counter-accusations fly back and forth, and no possibility of reconciliation appears on the horizon.

Here the practice of meditation can enable us to withstand such storms as well as to realise the wisdom of the saying from

Ecclesiastes: There is a time to embrace and a time not to embrace. When one is in the vortex of such a situation it is better to suggest a pause in the relationship, a time for silence rather than words, because given such intense pain words can all too often become as treacherous as brambles in a dark wood. If two people truly love each other then they should be able to accept such a time of withdrawal until the melodrama of the situation has waned. In Shakespeare's play *Cymbeline* Imogen says at one point, 'O Time, 'tis thou must untangle this, not I!' Through the practice of meditation we are able to look into the eye of the storm and wait for it to pass. And in the process we shall almost always see that neither of us is without fault. I would go further and say that if one values a relationship one should not be afraid to eat humble pie. I recall being in a situation in which someone I employed, who was also a friend, refused to answer my letters or return my telephone calls. This went on for several months until one day I knew that if I did not break this deadlock the situation would only worsen. As I drove to call on him there resounded in my head the words of the famous Shaker hymn, *Simple Gifts*, with its refrain, 'To bow and to bend we shan't be ashamed, To turn, turn, will be our delight. Till by turning, turning we come round right.' Those words, 'To bow and to bend we shan't be ashamed' I repeated over and over. When I arrived I walked straight in and said, 'I want to apologise. It was entirely my fault.'

It is at such times of stress that we often lose our keys, our wallet, or passport. Forgetting our keys and being locked out of our own home may perhaps be telling us that we feel locked out of our relationship, or that we don't want to go back inside the relationship. When we lose our keys or dream that we have lost our way it is important to heed these signals and take a closer look at what is happening in our lives: it is often at such times of fracture or loss that we are being challenged to reassemble the pieces of our own jigsaw.

In an essay, *Reporting from the Shore-line*, Michael Ford, a BBC journalist, describes how he once worked for a newspaper whose offices were only a few miles from the sea. The sub-editor, whose marriage had broken down, was often depressed and a difficult person with whom to deal. For months Michael Ford noticed that at lunchtime he would disappear from his office with his flask and sandwiches rather than join the rest of the staff in the local pub. Later on the sub-editor told him that every day he felt compelled to drive to the nearest beach and eat his sandwiches at the water's edge. He needed, he said, to look out at the distant horizon and reflect on his life. And this daily meditation on the beach always put him in a better mood for the afternoon. He was doing instinctively what Robert Frost described as 'taking time out for re-assembly'.

None of us can escape, at one time or another, the experience of being lost in a dark wood. As Helen Luke observes in her introduction to Dante's *Divine Comedy, Dark Wood to White Rose*, 'We cannot bypass the experience of Hell. And still less can we evade the long struggle of Purgatory through which we come to maturity in love.' Even when trapped in a maze there is always something for us to learn. The title of Martha Graham's dance-work, *Errand Into The Maze*, tells us this: that in entering the maze we have an errand, a task, and once it is accomplished we can then emerge from the maze or the dark wood. What we learn as we travel through the brambles of such dark places is who we are, where we have come from, and where we are going.

6

Waiting Patiently for the Autumn and Spring Rains

The practice of meditation leads us to an awareness that within each one of us is another landscape: it is like a country house with many rooms and attics, passages, gardens, woods, and wasteland. We shall in the course of our life become familiar with some of these rooms, many of which will be entered for the first time, while others remain locked – at least in this existence. But meditation is not a guided tour of a country house. Meditation is not intended as a form of self-analysis. Rather it is that the practice of stillness, of meditation, leads to an increased awareness of ourselves as well as of others, to a greater humility and an increased sense of humour. These last two points are important. All this talk, all these words I am using, can make us over-intense, a little too solemn, perhaps even precious, taking ourselves just a little bit too seriously. To be related to the *humus* (earth) will beget *hum*ility, and true humility ripens into *hum*our. We become less and less deceived about ourselves (and those selves are many); we have fewer illusions and therefore are more aware of other people as themselves and not as the carriers of our psychological projections. We become aware that many of the rooms within us are shabby, shoddy, even pretentious, while others, long untouched, when opened up and the shutters drawn to let in the sunlight, prove to contain unexpected treasures. In such rooms we discover unlived lives, unused talents, and much neglected business.

The stone which the builders ignored proves time and again to be the cornerstone we need. Meditation is one such stone.

When we feel frustrated and restless, finding no satisfaction in our work, our religion, and our relationships deadlocked, we still continue to do everything except this one thing: to stop, be still, and listen. We cannot imagine that by doing nothing, as it seems, we can achieve anything. And in the meantime our true Self lies neglected, that Self which has unsuspected powers of renewal. 'It is not what you are or have been that God looks at with His merciful eyes,' says the unknown author of *The Cloud of Unknowing*, 'but what you would be.' We stand at the door of our own house. We have but to knock and let ourselves in!

The capacity of the human spirit for renewal is endless. Meditation is very like the creative process in which artists can experience periods when no inspiration seems forthcoming. But from experience the artist knows that these are fallow periods. Although the surface seems barren, as blank as a field or garden in the mists and rain of November, he knows that underground the roots and bulbs are biding their time. Knowing this does not make the dark days of winter pass more quickly, and the artist, unlike the gardener or farmer, will often experience despair born of the fear that perhaps the sources of his creativity have dried up. Yet even the farmer is at the mercy of the elements. 'Be patient, then, my brothers, until the Lord (inspiration) comes. See how the farmer is patient as he waits for his land to produce precious crops. He waits patiently for the autumn and spring rains. And you also must be patient.' (St James 5: 7-8)

Yet for the artist, and for those who meditate, wisdom, always the fruit of experience, teaches us this patience. The spring does return in due season – though when it comes it may be an entirely new growth and not at all what we expected. As George Herbert wrote:

Who would have thought my shrivell'd heart
Could have recovered greenness? It was gone

Quite underground, as flowers depart
To feed their mother-root when they have blown;
Where they together
All the hard weather,
Dead to the world, keep house unknown.

I recall being in Finland, working at the National Theatre in Helsinki, throughout one March. Towards the end of the month the thaw of the long winter snows began. This was a time of ugliness in the city, with soot-coloured snow, sleet and puddles, and dark, crow-black buildings. In the parks as the last of the snows melted in the sun I saw, underneath, the crushed and anaemic grass, as drained of colour as the whitened faces of the 'winter' Finns who daily assembled on the steps of the cathedral in the middle of the day, standing with eyes closed and their pale faces uplifted to the returning sun. Yet one knew that within a short space of time the grass would spring up green and vivid once again in the sunshine, just as those pale faces would turn golden and become the faces of 'summer' Finns.

Time and again it can seem as though we will never recover from certain experiences that have battered us into defeat. Repeatedly in meditation it will seem as though the interior winter has no end. We sit alert, continuing to meditate, yet the weather never changes and we begin to doubt the efficacy of what we are doing. Gone are the days of warmth, of glowing devotion, of beatific experiences, of being on fire with love. We have become a bleak and wintry landscape.

The artist knows, however, that underneath, in the unconscious, seeds are stirring and then, one day, a new work is created. And we, too, one day look up from our meditating and are aware that, quite suddenly, we have moved on. Certain problems have fallen away, certain attitudes or prejudices have shifted or changed. A new awareness is born. If we really allow the creative forces their freedom, and if we willingly suffer the ignominy of knowing that, at such a time of winter, there is little we can do other than go on meditating, then it will take care of itself. Jesus said, 'It is good for you that I go away.' Winter is necessary to spring. All spiritual masters say the same thing, that such periods of bleakness are testing, as Prospero says to Miranda in Shakespeare's *The Tempest*:

> All thy vexations
> Were but trials of thy love, and thou
> Hast strangely stood the test.

 7

A Journey of the Spirit

If one accepts the proposition that man is essentially a religious person, as David Hay has advanced, then we have to acknowledge that unless we recover our capacity for religious awareness we will not be able to become fully human, remembering that the word 'religion' means a search for meaning. Whether the Churches can again provide a living experience of religion, it is clear that in many instances there is a sense of the centre falling apart and never was Yeats' poem, *The Second Coming*, more prophetic:

> Turning and turning in the widening gyre
> The falcon cannot hear the falconer;
> Things fall apart; the centre cannot hold;
> Mere anarchy is loosed upon the world,
> The blood-dimmed tide is loosed, and everywhere
> The ceremony of innocence is drowned;

The best lack all conviction, while the worst
Are full of passionate intensity.

Yet this may be only the sign of fundamental change.
If Christianity can be open in its encounters with the other
great religions of the world, then it may be able to satisfy the
surprising hunger for the things of the Spirit that is so often to
be found today outside the Churches. In *A Journey to Ladakh*
Andrew Harvey quotes the young Drukchen Rinpoche, and
in the following passage I would suggest the reader substitute
for the word 'Buddhist' the word 'Christian'. 'A true Buddhist
does not remain attached to one tradition or another. He is
grateful for what he can learn from the past, but he does not
remain addicted to its insights, even to its way of doing things.'
Buddhism, he says, will change, must change and in so doing
will reveal a new aspect of its truth, a new possibility in its
wisdom. 'Buddhism in the West will be very different in many
ways from Buddhism as the Tibetan tradition has interpreted
it, but why should we mourn that? We should welcome it.'
No society, no country, no world has a monopoly of spiritual
insight, of spiritual truth.

Sadly many Christians, perhaps even the majority, feel
threatened by any religious tradition other than their own.
They cannot acknowledge, let alone perceive, the wisdom
and the beauty of the Upanishads, the Sufi mystics and
especially the writings of Rumi, the sayings of Lao Tzu, the
teachings of the Hasid, or of the Buddha, nor see how it is
possible to be enriched by these insights and weave them
into their own lives as Christians. It is a way, however, that
has been pioneered by such individuals as Père de Foucauld,
Dom Bede Griffiths, Thomas Merton, Teilhard de Chardin,
Father Kadowaki SJ, Dom Déchanet, Dom Aelred Graham,
William Johnson SJ, Father Monchanin, Father Henri le
Saux (better known as Abhishiktananda, one of the great
mystics of the twentieth century) and many more. As Ursula

King observed in her study of Teilhard de Chardin, *Towards a New Mysticism* the emergence of a global society has brought with it the idea that we must develop a new consciousness and identity as world citizens, so that 'we perhaps need a new kind of world believer who can meaningfully relate to the perspective of more than one religious tradition, and thereby find a deep enrichment.'

Each of the individuals above (the majority, interestingly, are Roman Catholic) is among the pioneers of such a new spirituality and represents a genuinely open religious quest, one that cuts across major religious and denominational differences. On 10 December 1968, on the last day of his life, Thomas Merton spoke these words: 'I believe that by openness to Buddhism, Hinduism, and to these great Asiatic traditions, we stand a wonderful chance of learning more about the potentiality of our own traditions, because they have gone, from the natural point of view, so much deeper into this than we have.' Fundamentally the search is for a deeper fulfilment of life; not for *well-being* but rather, as Teilhard de Chardin expressed it, for *more-being*.

Throughout the ages women and men have been intuitively aware of an inner centre, of a Self beyond the self. The Greeks called it man's inner daemon; in Egypt they spoke of it as the Ba-soul; the Romans referred to it as the genius native to every human being. Quakers speak of it as the inner light which is available to all who learn how to centre down within themselves; while Carl Jung referred to it as the Self, meaning by this the essential identity at the heart of each human being as opposed to the petty tyrant of the ego, or the self with a small 's'. Increasingly today people are discovering once again that it is from within themselves that they must find the answers if they are to achieve a meaningfulness in their lives. As Jesus said, 'The Kingdom of Heaven is within.' All who begin to listen to the voice within learn that they have entered upon a journey of the spirit in search of answers to those eternal questions: Who am I? Where have I come from? Where am I going? And having once heard the call, it is enough to set out on the journey.

Who is my Teacher?

In my home in Wales I have two watercolour paintings done for me by an American-Chinese artist, Cheng Hsui. The first shows a Zen monk with a tall staff setting forth on a journey into a thick wall of mist. This seems to me an apt image of the practice of meditation for in meditation we enter, of necessity, a cloud of un-knowing in which we learn to let go of all our knowing, of all dreams and imaginings, of all thought. It is a matter of being rather than doing anything other than following the breath or repeating a mantra. As Lao Tzu says, 'For a vessel to be filled it must first be emptied!' The second painting shows the same monk, seated now, cross-legged, on the edge of a precipice, gazing into the void below which is swirling with mist. This image reminds us how, repeatedly, in our practice we are assailed from time to time by a vortex of memories, resentments, daydreams, yearnings. We learn to acknowledge them and then let them go, returning to focusing on the breath, or on the mantra. Occasionally, however, the mists clear and for a few moments we may glimpse the valley below and the mountain ranges beyond. And in that moment we experience the one-ness of all creation, what the great physicist David Bohm referred to as 'the Implicate Order' in which everything in the universe affects everything else because each is a part of the same unbroken whole. Everything

is connected to everything else. As the character played by
James Dean in the film *Rebel Without a Cause*, cries out to his
mother, 'But, Mam, we are all involved!' Of course this is also
the central teaching of mysticism: that all Reality is One. It is
this realisation that explains why many today are searching
less for theory or theology and more for what in Asia is
termed 'practice': hence the growing attraction in the West
for Buddhism and other forms of meditation. It is interesting
to note that at the Asian Synod of Roman Catholic Bishops
held in Rome in 1998 several Bishops spoke of Asia's difficulty
with Western theology. Whereas the West uses a plethora of
words, Asia prefers silence. One Bishop spoke of the Western
penchant for analysing, separating, dividing; whereas Asia, on
the other hand, is contemplative, seeing God in all things.

Of course we can experience this one-ness of all things
outside of meditation and for many it can come when they are
alone with Nature. There is a very moving illustration of this in
Joseph Jaworski's autobiographical book, *Synchronicity: the Inner
path of Leadership*. Jaworski was a leading American attorney
who, after the break-up of his first marriage, began to reflect
on the larger purpose of his life and so he decided to take time
out by going backpacking in the Grand Teton Mountains.
There, 11,000ft up, near Hurricane Pass, in mid-October, he
gets up early one morning in order to fish in a stream. As he
walks along, suddenly in front of him a beautiful ermine pops
up out of the deep snow, her eyes looking directly into his.
She sits there staring straight at him. She turns to go but stops,
turns round again, and takes another long look at him. Then
she begins. She jumps up into the air and does a huge flip,
and looks into his eyes again, as if to say, 'What did you think
about that?' She does this same trick for him three or four
times, each time cocking her head to the side and looking at
him as if to ask for his approval. He stands there, transfixed.
He begins smiling and cocking his head in the same direction
as hers. This goes on for a long time. There, together, he feels

at one with the ermine. Finally, when she has finished, she turns around once more to look at him, before going down into the snow again and disappearing. He stays in that spot for a long time, reflecting on what he recognises as a profound experience. 'We communicated, that ermine and I, and for those few moments I experienced what I can only describe as a kind of transcendence of time and a feeling of one-ness with all the universe. The encounter with the ermine was so important to me because it was the first time I had directly experienced the inter-relatedness of the universe.'

Anything, and anyone, can be our Teacher: a child or a stranger, our enemy or critic, but also an animal. It is interesting to reflect how many of the Saints are associated with a particular animal, from St Jerome and his lion, St Francis and the wolf of Gubbio, to St Kevin and his blackbird, St Luke and the ox. Thinking of how animals can be our teachers I recall a story told to me by a friend who is a psychotherapist. He had a client, a man with AIDS, who was so tense with fear that his whole body was rigid and he found it difficult to talk. Then at one session, when the therapist had forgotten to close the door of his consulting room, his cat entered and leaped onto the man's lap. Instinctively the man began to caress the cat and with this he began to relax and to talk freely. The cat, in this instance, was indeed a catalyst! Teaching can come in many forms.

9

Swimming in the Ocean of Love

Using a mantra, as opposed to following the breath, has been used as a form of meditation for many centuries. The mantra is a sacred word, the eternal Logos, that 'word beyond recall' of which the Psalmist speaks, vibrating in the universe. It is any word or phrase that enshrines the essence of that towards which we gravitate in the depths of our being, and which we may choose to call God, or Allah. For the Hindu the most sacred of all names is the word 'Om'. Many adherents of the world's major religions, from Judaism and Christianity to Islam and Hinduism, put the power of the Holy Name into practice through the repetition of spiritual formulae containing a holy name or a divine attribute. For the Sufi, the devout Muslim, who aspires to remember God in every moment, with each and every breath, it can be a phrase such as 'There is no God but God'. Perhaps the most famous example from Hinduism is the mantra 'Om mane padme hum' while in the Orthodox Church we find the mantra, 'Lord Jesus Christ, Son of the Living God, have mercy on me a sinner.' Mystics of all traditions testify that the mantra, systematically repeated over a period of years, can permeate our consciousness and transform our character. In some Sufi orders, as also in certain Buddhist practices, it is chanted at group meetings when it becomes a very powerful experience. But many prefer a silent invocation. As one Sufi master wrote, 'God is silence and is most easily reached in silence.' It is said that Muhammed when asked by his cousin and son-in-law Ali the shortest way to God, replied, 'Ali, always repeat the name of God in solitary places.'

By continually repeating the sacred word or phrase it will begin to resonate within us so that, waking in the night, we will find that it begins to sound of its own accord like a tolling bell. Through this repetition the mantra begins to work in the unconscious, slowly transforming our mental, psychological and physical selves. As the contemporary Sufi teacher Llewellyn Vaughan-Lee has written, 'Spiritual life is a process of inner transformation, like seeds planted deep within the earth, the spiritual processes slowly germinate and may take years to flower into consciousness.' As we allow the mantra to repeat itself throughout the day and whenever we wake in the night so this practice will deepen in us an awareness of that other dimension which we may choose to call God – the label itself is unimportant – and, like St Paul, we become aware that it is in this dimension that 'we live and move and have our being.' The ocean of Love is all around us and all we have to do is to swim in it! But first we have to learn how to swim which is why we practise these simple techniques which have been proved and tested across the centuries by all the major religions.

Sometimes an individual may deliberately choose a form of words that applies to a particular situation. One friend whose wife developed Parkinson's Disease, realising the demands that lay before him with such an illness, found himself using the Buddhist mantra: 'That I may be filled with loving kindness.' Whatever the words, we are not meditating on them in an analytical or discursive manner but, by repeating them over and over we are allowing them to sink into our subconscious until they are embedded in us, rather like those sticks of rock bought at the seaside which would have the word 'Blackpool' all the way through them. In this way the words and their deeper meaning begin to resonate within us like the beating of our heart.

One woman, a registered nurse, a vicar's wife, mother of three daughters, who has been meditating for thirteen years, and who has suffered from episodes of severe depression and obsessive compulsive disorder (OCD) since early adolescence, writes:

> Thousands of people all over the world must be able to testify to meditation holding, helping and re-shaping them in everyday life and also in the midst of personal suffering. At its worst, a bout of depression and OCD means for me that I am constantly, inwardly, bombarded with unwelcome, intrusive and very unpleasant and frightening thoughts. Some people check locks endlessly. I ruminate on torturing thoughts. At times, when in crisis, I have felt like I have lost 'me' and all that gives me a sense of self-hood. During my meditation periods, using the mantra, I have clung on in the darkness, doing all that I can manage – which is to faithfully return to the mantra, trusting that although I don't know who I am, God does.

> I want to thank God for John Main, the Benedictine monk, who founded the World Christian Meditation Movement, and many others who have re-discovered the immense treasures of contemplative prayer, and also to encourage anyone reading this who suffers from mental illness – which has its unique challenges – to carry on in and through the darkness with naked and often blind trust. By the grace of God, and for me, especially through meditation, we can access the love and power we need to help us and hold us and re-make us.

In Islam, as has been noted, there is the practice of repeating the name of 'Allah'; in Hinduism that of 'Ram' or one of the other names of God; in the Kabbala tradition of Hasidic Judaism that of 'Jahveh', and in Christianity that of 'Jesus'. And here it is intriguing to conjecture that Jesus' own mantra may well have been the Aramaic word 'Abba'. All Aramaic words carry several meanings rather as Chinese ideograms do. And so the word Abba can mean an earthly father, but also father and mother, and beyond that, the source and origin of all things.

And so as a Christian I often find myself beginning the Lord's prayer in this way: Abba, Father-Mother, Source and Origin of all things, hallowed be Thy name'

For the Jewish people of the Old Testament the name of God was not to be written or uttered, and he remained a remote, jealous and angry figure. It was Jesus who taught that this was an anthropomorphic projection and that God was much more: that God was Love. In the end, as in this Sufi poem, it is Love that draws us:

I thought of You so often
That I completely became You.
Little by little You drew near
And slowly but slowly I passed away.

 10

A Perfected Life

It can happen that a mantra will well up from a person's unconscious and if that happens one must heed it. For me it happened with a friend who, when she died in 2007, was only a few months short of ninety-nine. She was born into a world almost unrecognisable now except in the pages of Kilvert's Diaries where, indeed, her mother's family, the Crichtons of Wyecliffe at Hay, are frequently mentioned. It was in 1907 that her father, George Powell, became Rector of Dorstone in the Golden Valley in Herefordshire, as his father had been before him. The following year he married Kathleen Maud Crichton and they had three children: Ann, the eldest, Llewelyn and Mary. He was one of the last hunting, fishing and shooting parsons – squarsons, as they were called – part squire, part parson. He would never accept payment from his own parishioners for funerals or weddings, and would try to visit everyone at least twice a year.

Ann eventually went off to London to become a teacher but returned in the 1950s to nurse her mother. She was a keen botanist and ornithologist and a much respected member of the Radnorshire Society. With the hands of a gardener and the feet of a walker she travelled miles in search of rare plants and birds. For over forty-five years she was also, as a devout Anglican, a member of the Church's Fellowship for Spiritual and Psychical Studies. Right up until her ninety-eighth birthday she still lived alone in a small cottage at Great Oak, Eardisley in Herefordshire, driving once a week to Hay-on-Wye to shop and have her hair done. She was a great reader and her letters, written in her fine calligraphy, were always full of interest and concern for others. In one, dated 29 April 2006, she wrote, 'In the gardens the magnolias are magnificent; my white cherry has never been so lovely. And the hedgerows are so white with blackthorn and cherry. I don't remember seeing so much white showing up in the hedgerows just beginning to green. Driving back from Hay on Thursday I saw a house martin collecting mud from a roadside puddle. What a wonder – flying thousands of miles and then having to build a nest with tiny beakfuls of mud. I was singing quietly in my heart to myself:

Praise to the Lord Almighty,
The King of Creation,
O my soul, praise Him for He is thy health and salvation.

Our friendship deepened over the years. Then in August, about three years ago, shortly before I was due to have angioplasty surgery, as I stepped out one afternoon from her cottage, after being with her, there came entirely unbidden into my head these words: *God is present. God is here. God is now.*

A week later, as I lay in the operating theatre, quietly repeating this mantra to myself, something very dramatic happened, to the amazement of the cardiologist and his assistants who were shouting, 'Wow! Look at that! I have never seen that before!' Suddenly the blood clot, the scar tissue and the plaque all blew away, leaving a clear artery, so that there was no need to carry out the angioplasty. Later I shared all this with Ann and thereafter these words became part of our simple ritual when I was leaving. Holding hands, we would say these words together. A year later when she was rushed to Hereford Hospital and her niece urged me to go at once as she was not expected to live, I found her lying quietly, her eyes closed, saying these words over and over to herself. They had become for her, as also for me, a special mantra.

On one occasion she said, 'I feel so helpless. There is so little I can do.' I replied, 'Ann, you don't have to do anything, except *be*!' And I thought of the Emily Dickinson poem, a copy of which she had sent me several years earlier:

The props assist the house
Until the house is built,
And then the props withdraw –
And adequate, erect,
The house supports itself;
Ceasing to recollect
The auger and the carpenter.
Just such a retrospect
Hath the perfected life,
A past of plank and nail,
And slowness – then the scaffolds drop
Affirming it a soul.

What one saw in Ann during her last years was such a perfected life. She no longer had to do anything but be, while to be in her presence was gift enough. And so now, at intervals throughout the day and whenever I wake in the night, I quietly repeat the mantra that came to me that afternoon when standing outside her cottage in Herefordshire.

 II

The Lonely Place

There was a time in my early twenties when, as a Catholic, I used regularly to serve the Sunday Mass at the Carmelite Monastery in Golders Green, London. The Prioress, Sister Ann of the Holy Spirit, who took me under her wing, once showed me photographs of the interior of the monastery. I was much struck by one in particular, showing an archway in their cloisters painted round which were the words: 'In Carmel and at the Judgment I am alone with God.' It reminded me that loneliness is essential to the human condition and each of us has to learn how to come to terms with it. Learning to meditate is part of this process. I think it was the Venerable Chogyam Trungpa, one of those who brought Buddhism to the West, who said that meditation should be boring – as boring as possible. Because only in intense boredom are all our habitual responses and concepts dissolved. The mind has a terror of boredom and loneliness for it suspects that by means of such an intense experience another level of reality may be reached that will threaten its pretensions. And so, rather than face monotony, boredom and loneliness, we fill up every conceivable hour with activity in order to prop up our fragile sense of identity and imagined usefulness. Social, domestic, professional, sensual and trivial activities crowd out the possibility of any empty spaces within us, or of an encounter, like that of Jacob, with a dark angel who has come to wound us so that we may be healed. We are so impatient for activity and do not know how to contain our restlessness within a nave of silence. It is a very common hazard among the caring professions, from doctors and priests to counsellors, healers, therapists, who often are so busy with other people's problems that, quite unknowingly, they have no time for their own problems and therefore evade that ultimate appointment with their own selves.

It is when we are alone that we have to confront, as Emily Dickinson put it, 'Ourself behind ourself concealed'. The memory of failures, betrayals, woundings, well up and if we simply suppress them they will only renew their attacks. However, although in meditation they may well up as distractions, this is not the time for confronting them. If we can hold firmly to the centre, even while assailed by our many selves, something else happens slowly over the months, even years. Gently, barely discernible, our souls and our psyches are purified. The silence of meditation, provided we truly surrender ourselves to it, will loosen psychological knots and dissolve subconscious coagulations, draining away those secret poisons that invade our psyches.

Loneliness, I repeat, is central to the human condition. It is the secret plague that, for all our technological and material progress, invades and attacks Western society more insidiously than any germ warfare. No husband, wife, lover, friend or work can ultimately satisfy the depths of loneliness in each of us. No lover can satisfy such hunger: indeed, in many cases it drives them away. And so those words of St Augustine continue to resound across the centuries: 'Thou, O Lord, hast made us for Thyself and our hearts are restless until they find their rest in Thee.' All those who go from partner to partner, divorce to divorce, job to job, distraction to distraction, are in search of a mirage. We must therefore be prepared to go apart into a lonely place. We all live in a fragmented and disturbing time, one in which it is hard to keep our spiritual balance. And therefore, if we are to be of use to others, the greater the need to meditate.

The Rinproche, the Priest, the Iman, the Rabbi, the Swami, the Sheik, are each of them guardians of another order of reality and it may well be that today it is the contemplative side of their vocation that is the most important to nurture. Paradoxically it is those who have learned to be alone with their aloneness who draw others to them. The Desert Fathers, the holy men and women of India in their caves and ashrams, Mother Julian in her cell in Norwich, Père de Foucauld in the desert, Abhishiktananda in his cave at Arunachala, the Little Brothers and Sisters of Jesus in their cells in city and country, all hermits and anchorites everywhere, and many ordinary people, speak to our society in a way that is urgently needed. Solitary in their caves, alone with the Alone, they draw us gently to our true home as surely as migrating birds return to the place of their origin.

12

The Maker of Souls

There was a time when I used to do long lecture tours of America. Always, in spite of the warmth of hospitality, I found these very lonely times. One morning in Colorado Springs I took down from a shelf in the house where I was staying a volume of the poems of Emily Dickinson. It opened on a particular poem, one line of which immediately caught my eye: 'Loneliness – the maker of the soul', and I thought, Wow! She knew. Here is the actual verse:

I fear me – this is Loneliness –
The Maker of the soul
Its Caverns and its Corridors
Illuminate or seal.

For the greater part of her life Emily Dickinson chose to be a recluse, though this did not mean that she cut herself off from the outside world. Indeed her letters reveal how intense was her involvement with other people, but she needed solitude in order to nurture her gift. The first stirrings of this need began to appear in her adolescence when she was subjected to a form of collective pressure commonly experienced by her contemporaries at that period of intense religious revivals. She found herself faced with the demands of her social group in Amherst to openly accept the Christian faith. 'Christ is calling everyone here,' she wrote to a friend. 'All my companions have answered, even my darling Vinnie (her sister) believes she loves and trusts Him, and I am standing alone in rebellion, and growing very careless. Abby, Mary, Jane, and farthest of all my Vinnie have been seeking, and they believe they have found; I can't tell you *what* they have found, but *they* think it is something precious. I wonder if it *is*?' Increasingly she found excuses for staying away from the services. 'They will all go but me to the usual meeting house, to hear the usual sermon; the inclemency of the storm so kindly detaining me.' She only knew that in silence and in solitude she must go on seeking 'oppositely for the Kingdom of Heaven.'

So deep was her instinct to be her self rather than conform that for several years she endured a continuing conflict. 'I am out with lanterns looking for myself,' she wrote at this period, while many of her poems of this time contain the image of a boat adrift. Then in 1859, when this conflict was at its most intense, she suddenly began to see that instead of fearing shipwreck she should set her sails towards the open seas, and she came to write what for me are among her most haunting lines:

> Exultation is the going
> Of an inland soul to sea,
> Past the houses, past the headlands,
> Into deep Eternity.

That she is implying life after death here is doubtful, rather it signifies the wholeness of life to be found in the inner world. And so, slowly but surely, she found her true Self. It was by living her own experience through to the utmost, by being true to her own destiny, that she passed the limits of the purely personal and touched something much larger and deeper, and had experience of that 'more-life' of which Teilhard de Chardin spoke, and for which we all yearn. She came to realise that in the depths of her own self, depths which at first she feared, lay the treasure that is there for each of us to find. In one of my workshops at Colorado College I once invited my students to write a prayer 'to a known or unknown God'. This is what one of them, Dickson Musselwhite, wrote:

> With the unsecuring sea stretching
> Before me,
> To mystery
> I make my pledge.
> To search
> To swim
> To dive as deep as I can.

> With the unsecuring sea stretching
> Before me,
> To mystery
> I give my thanks.

For you I am thankful
With you I am.
Without you I am not.

For all those who, like Dickson, like Emily, have the courage to make a commitment, who are prepared to search, to dive as deep as they can, they will always find the sunken treasure hidden deep within themselves and, like Walt Whitman, be enabled to say, 'Now in a moment I know what I am for and a thousand songs spring to life within my breast!'

Recent statistics show that more people are lonely today than ever before. This is due in part to the long hours which many have to work and which leave little time for forging relationships, or else leaves people too tired to make the effort, especially in a family where both parents work and bring up children. In major cities in America you can now sign up for 'cuddle parties' which offer experiences of non-sexual hugging for those starved of physical contact with others. Nor is it surprising, therefore, that more and more meditation groups are springing up like clusters, for such groups offer the kind of structure and sense of community that many have lost or never even known.

 13

Dealing with the Bluebottles

On some days the time set aside for meditation will seem interminable. It can happen both to the beginner and to someone who may have been meditating for years. When this happens we should not cut short the time set aside but, rather, open our eyes, look at the clock, acknowledge our restlessness and then go back into the meditation. Even if this occurs every few minutes there is no need to be discouraged. One needs great patience. T.H. White in his short book *The Goshawk*, describing training the bird, observes, 'I saw now that I must learn to feed him with diligent and minute observation. Suddenly I realised that this was the secret of all training.'

Inevitably thoughts, worries, distractions will distract us like a bluebottle. The actress Maggie Smith once said of an actor, 'He's like a bluebottle, all over the place. You never know where he's going to be next, and he never stops long enough so you can swot him!' And I recall how once when I was working in New York and each week used to visit Dr Masha Rollins, a Jungian analyst, on one occasion I was disturbed by a bluebottle in her room and rolling up a newspaper got up to try and catch it. Quietly Masha Rollins said, 'Let it be! It has been here all winter.' It was then that I began to learn to come to terms with my own bluebottle thoughts.

Each time the bluebottle thoughts distract us when we are meditating we must disengage ourselves and return to saying our mantra or following the breath. As Lao Tzu wrote, 'I do my utmost to attain emptiness. I hold firmly to stillness. Returning to one's roots is known as stillness.' Sometimes, however, thoughts or images may arise which are not necessarily distractions but well up from the unconscious like fish rising to the surface. Sometimes, out of the stillness of the meditation the solution to a problem may present itself. We acknowledge it and then put it to one side to be reflected upon after our meditation. The river flows past but we remain on the bank. There is the river. There is the current ever flowing. There is the angler waiting. And the river and the angler are separate but one. The angler waits for the Great Fish.

Once, leading a retreat at an old country house in Suffolk, on a cold day in March, a group of us were sitting, wrapped in blankets, around a large ornamental pool in the garden. Our meditation was to gaze at the pool in which the grey-blue sky was reflected, its stillness disturbed at first only by the passage of a bird in the sky, reflected in the water: a crow winging its way to the nearby wood. Then, beneath the surface of the watery mirror, among the dark roots of the water lilies, we became aware of a large carp moving slowly, appearing and disappearing. And so at the heart of every Pool the Great Fish lies waiting. But we cannot command him. He appears of his own will and in the same manner he disappears. When the mirror reflects nothing but the empty sky, even then he is there, deep beneath the surface. And so we sat on, watching and waiting. We saw the mirror change colour as the sky became green and then, softly, out of the sky, snowflakes began to fall and we watched as snowflake after snowflake met its image in the water and was dissolved in the Great Pool, becoming one with the Infinite. 'When you fix your heart on one point,' said the Buddha, 'then nothing is impossible for you.' At the heart of every pool the Great Fish lies waiting.

What is it that leads people to want to learn about meditation? In the main it is because, in one way or another, they feel that their present form of life is unsatisfactory. Without such a need, such an ache of the heart, such a yearning of the spirit, nothing new can come into being. But for something new to emerge we have to learn how to let go of our ego, for only to the extent that we learn not to take ourselves as the measure of all things, or assume that we are the masters and mistresses of our fate, can we grow. And the process can be very humbling at times, even daunting, as the ego protests. All who follow the path of meditation, whether Christian, Muslim, Buddhist, Hindu, or agnostic, will at times encounter an emptiness, a bleakness, so that we begin to question why we are even bothering to meditate. And for those who believe in a Deity it may seem as though God does not exist and at such times we hear the archetypal cry of all mankind in those words of Jesus on the cross: My God, my God, why have you forsaken me!

In what is perhaps the most remarkable passage in her spiritual autobiography, St Thérèse of Lisieux speaks of the absolute and unrelenting quality of darkness which threatened to overwhelm her in the last eighteen months of her life. 'I got so tired of the darkness all round me,' she said. And we know that for some forty years, throughout the most demanding years of her life, Mother Teresa of Calcutta ceased to have any sense of God, experiencing no spiritual consolations whatever. Yet this did not mean that she ceased to believe or continue to spend hours each day in meditation and prayer, for this was the source of her amazing energy and activity. C.S. Lewis rightly observed, 'Of course the presence of God is not the same as the sense of the presence of God. The latter may be due to imagination, the former may be attended with no "spiritual consolations". The sense of the presence is a super-added gift for which we give thanks when it comes, and that is all.'

In other words, as the Buddha said, 'Begin – and then continue.' And so we continue with our practice, day in, day out, whether we feel like it or not. Once we have begun to meditate we have no choice but to continue. In a sense we are on a journey that will lead us across barren deserts, impenetrable jungles and wild places, as well as oases of great calm. It is the same instinct that drove such explorers as Columbus or Scott or Galileo. Learning to endure the void, the darkness, the emptiness, enables us to face up to ourselves. It strips us of all illusions and enables us to let go of all expectations. I once thought to have carved on my gravestone the words: *Hope for all things, expect nothing.* Meditation teaches us an ultimate objectivity, placing everything *sub species aeternitatis*, in an eternal perspective. As Virginia Woolf wrote on the last page of her journal: 'Observe. Observe perpetually. Observe the onset of age.' Each setback, each failure, each shame, each pain, every betrayal, sorrow or loss, must be looked at, confronted, and above all, fathomed, so that we may learn what each has to teach us. As Rumi says in his poem *The Guest House*, 'Be grateful for whoever comes, because each has been sent as a guide from beyond.' Ultimately we are alone and yet, paradoxically, not alone for there is always Another who leads and watches over us. It is this Other who is our Guide on the journey of meditation and of life itself.

Waiting for a Door to Open

Neither prayer nor meditation can be taught by books. A book such as this, a few words, perhaps only a single phrase, may act as a signpost, no more. One can read about meditation but above all one has to experience it. One cannot know about love until one has been in love. And just as one can stand in front of a painting, or read a poem, or hear a certain piece of music, and nothing happens, its essence eluding us, so, too, in meditation. We stand in front of a painting by Paul Klee, or Stanley Spencer, or Mark Rothko, trying to see something in it. There must be, we feel, something there since clearly others have found something in these works, and yet nothing clicks for us. And so we may choose to come back again, and even several times, to look at the same painting, hear the same piece of music, until one day a door opens and we enter the landscape of the painter or of the composer. We share in their vision. I remember Robert Frost describing how, as a poet, he would catch *sight* of something, perhaps a tuft of grass, or a birch tree, or a falling leaf, and he would have an *insight* into it, and then proceed to write a poem that would *excite* the reader to share in his insight. And so it is with the practice of meditation. There is a story about the great Shibli who used to visit the illustrious Thauri. The master was sitting so still that not a hair of him moved, and Shibli asked him, 'Where did you learn such stillness?' and Thauri replied, 'From my cat. He was watching a mouse-hole with even greater concentration than you have seen me.'

In these periods of waiting we should not expect to feel anything, nor should we look for results; otherwise we shall be like those lovers who are so unsure of themselves that they are always demanding assurances and reassurances, like a nervous gardener who, having planted bulbs in the winter, is forever digging them up to see how they are faring. We are so accustomed to what F. Mathias Alexander called 'end-gaining' that we find it very difficult not to be *doing* something. But in meditation a vessel can only be filled when first it has been emptied, as has already been observed. 'In the pursuit of the Way' says Lao Tzu, 'one does less and less every day. One does less and less until one does nothing at all, and when one does nothing at all, then there is nothing that can be undone.' He is not saying we should be lazy or passive. We must continue to lead busy, full lives, but when we go apart to meditate, or pray, we must learn to be still and wait upon the silence. And the more we practise the more will this silence and this stillness invade our whole being so that, however busy or active our lives, there will be at the centre this stillness.

The world about us is visible to us. What we can see with our own eyes, touch with our own hands, we can observe, verify and draw deductions from; but the world invisible, the reality beyond this present reality, which we cannot physically see or touch: how to verify that? There is no way, scientifically or intellectually, that we can come by such knowledge, for it is knowledge of another order. No one can be argued into a knowledge of God. No one can be talked into falling in love. Love remains an experience. And so in the silence of meditation there will come a knowledge that has nothing to do with questionnaires or encyclopaedias; a knowledge that cannot be proved scientifically or even pinned down into words – and yet it is a knowledge of unshaken and unshakeable surety. There is, as others have observed, scientific knowledge; there is intellectual knowledge, but there is intuitive, or contemplative knowledge, something that all artists know, and even great scientists such as Einstein.

Many people shy away from the idea of a wordless activity such as meditation because it represents a challenge, just as some people shy away from a commitment to love, and of course the two are very much the same. For both in love and in meditation one commits one's self to the unknown. And, just as the most loving relationships can have their boring patches when we can even feel out of love with each other and want to end it all, so, too, we can be tempted to give up the practice of meditation. However, we learn to take no notice of such patches other than to register, in meditation as in love, that we are moving through a dry season. We persevere in love, enduring the occasional pain and boredom, slowly building up a discipline that will enable us to endure rougher weather and more violent storms. Thus in time, as in those human relationships over which we have laboured, we become like a tree that has been battered by many storms but whose roots go deep.

We have to work at everything.

15

Stay in the Root of your Dream

The wisdom of the unconscious often reaches us through our dreams, and in a dream, a disembodied voice is usually the voice of the Higher Self. Sufism, alone of all the spiritual traditions today, stresses the importance of dreams and of the psychological aspects of the spiritual journey. As the contemporary Sufi teacher, Llewellyn Vaughan-Lee writes: 'Dreams are like mirrors in which we see ourselves. They reflect back our hidden self. And when we wake, our dreams can be a doorway through which we can walk back into this inner world. During the night, when the conscious mind is asleep, the heart is able to tell its story through the medium of dreams. Such dreams, like myths, are the poems of the soul.' It is no wonder, therefore, that Rumi, one of the great Sufi poets and mystics, wrote, 'Stay in the root of your dream. Don't climb out on intellectual branches!' One should treat a dream as one would a poem or any work of art. A superficial reading of a poem will only reveal the superficial. We have to live with a work of art, allowing it to work upon our unconscious, and so it is with certain dreams.

And so I awoke one morning from a dream that was so powerful that I immediately closed my eyes and went back into it in order to stay there as long as possible. In the dream I was walking down the main street of a small country town with the actress, and friend, Jane Lapotaire. I had the impression that we had both come from a place of such deep silence, a silence in which insights float to the surface as they sometimes can in meditation. It was very early in the

morning. There was no one about and it was all very still and
hushed, like the moments before dawn. We came to a corner
where I observed an old church, twelfth century, which had
once been a Catholic church and was now a Quaker Meeting
House. On the door was a circular handle carved in wood
in the shape of a rose. I intimated to Jane – no words were
spoken: we seemed to communicate telepathically – that we
should enter the Meeting for worship, but she indicated that
we should go on, that we should stay out in the open.

At the end of the street, on the opposite side, I could see
an arch leading to an Oxford College and my thought was
that I would like to show Jane this ancient place of learning.
But now she was leaning her head against the wall of a house,
listening intently to the silence, and I realised that I was meant
to do the same. There was such a freshness in the air, like an
early morning in the Mediterranean, presaging a day of great
heat. The silence was intense and the air so pure. On waking
I thought of Keats' lines:

> What little town by river or sea-shore
> Or mountain built with peaceful citadel
> Is emptied of this folk this pious morn?

The lines, of course, are from his *Ode to a Grecian Urn* which
ends significantly, with these words:

> Beauty is truth, truth beauty – that is all
> Ye know on earth, and all ye need to know.

Frequently since that dream, indeed increasingly so, I have
returned to that place of silence beyond silence. Of course, as
someone who has had many years of analysis, I am aware of
much else in the dream that has a personal resonance. Why is
the twelfth-century Catholic church now a Meeting House
for the Society of Friends? Why is the wooden handle on

the door carved in the shape of a rose? Why is the anima, as personified by Jane Lapotaire, saying to me: Don't go inside. Stay out in the open? Clearly what the dream is saying is what Rumi is saying in his poem: Stay in the root of your dream, don't climb out on intellectual branches. Listen to what the silence is telling you. Listen to what the anima, your soul, is telling you. Follow her example and listen. Across the way is the arch leading to the ancient knowledge of universities, while behind you is the twelfth-century church now a place for listening. But stay in the open. Be still and listen. There is scientific knowledge; there is intellectual knowledge; and there is contemplative knowledge. It is this last which will lead you into an awareness of, and a deeper understanding of, what is meant by spirituality.

Life, says Rumi, is a journey back to God. And if God is everywhere then we must be open to whenever and wherever God appears. We cannot limit the experience of God to any one set of dogmas or teachings even when they are claimed to be 'revealed teachings'. We cannot exclude the sacred beliefs and worship of others, for wherever we find goodness there, also, is God. 'He that is not against me,' said Jesus, 'is for me.' This means that we have to sit lightly to our institutions. It does not mean that we belittle them, only that we do not make idols of them. As Father Daniel O'Leary has written: 'The moment the Churches begin to believe in themselves more than in the Spirit entrusted to them, believing that they are chosen where others are not, then they are confusing institutional elitism with working for the Kingdom.'

And so some of us are called to stay outside, to stay in the open and listen.

16

The Open-Eyed Meditation

Having found our way to a particular form of meditation it is important to stay with it for a discipline of practice is essential. But, at the same time, we must not turn our form of meditation into an idol. It can happen that the time may come when the spirit is urging us to move in a different direction, to let down our nets into the deep. However, there are some individuals whose home life and work situation is so complicated, and who have long journeys to and from work, that they have little time, space or energy in which to meditate, and yet they are aware that this is the one thing they most need. What can they do?

It was for one such man who worked in the Foreign Office that I devised what I have come to call The Open-Eyed Meditation, and have since taught; a form of meditation that attempts to integrate the inner and outer worlds in which we live. I suggested that he take the words 'Thou, O Lord, art in the midst of us' and say them mentally, over and over, while keeping his eyes open as he walked to get the train in the morning, being aware of his surroundings, of the other people travelling on the train; aware of animals, buildings, the quality of light, of the weather, knowing that God is in everything. And then at intervals throughout the day, perhaps when dealing with a difficult colleague, that he keep repeating these words mentally. While nurturing our inner flame we need also to look with open eyes at everything; not only at the outer world but also at our prejudices, our animosities, our judgmental attitudes towards others, our resistances, our laziness, to see how egoistic most of us are, how we manipulate others to get our way.

Looking in but also looking out. So many of us dash through each day without stopping to look about us: to observe the pigeon on the railway platform scrabbling for crumbs, the tired woman in front of us returning home after a night shift, or a fractious child: for all the world is my neighbour. We are all involved. It is no good shutting our eyes twice a day in meditation if it is regarded as a retreat from the reality that is all around us. 'The wide world is all about you,' says a character in Tolkien's *The Lord of the Rings*, 'You can fence yourselves in but you cannot ever fence it out.'

Abu Said ibn Abi-l-Khayr also said, 'The perfect mystic is not an ecstatic devotee lost in contemplation of Oneness, nor a saintly recluse shunning all commerce with mankind, but "the true saint" goes in and out amongst people and eats and sleeps with them and buys and sells in the market and marries and takes part in social intercourse, and never forgets God in a single moment.' And so, with open eyes, repeating the mantra, we go about our work, ever aware of that other presence in our midst. God is not only in the deepest part of each one of us, in the innermost recesses of our being, but in the whole of creation.

It is at this point when I am leading a meditation retreat that I usually invite those present to go out into the streets for half an hour, keeping their eyes open, and all the time saying mentally, over and over, the words 'Thou, O Lord, art in the midst of us.' I say, 'If you meet someone you know, don't hurry away. Be aware of them. So often in accidental meetings there is a hidden purpose which all too often we fail to see or to respond to. O Lord, Thou art in the midst of us.' Our practice should permeate every aspect of our daily life, whether it is washing up after a meal, making love, or taking a child to school. God is in the midst of us.

The practice of meditation is the keeping of an appointment with ourselves, with all mankind, with all creation, with God. We may be in a crowded office, harassed by people, feeling ourselves stretched to the limit, yet we remain aware of others as part of the same eternal pattern, that God is in our midst. And so gradually we become more aware of the hidden sub-text in every meeting and we begin to hear the words of secret silence. We begin to experience what Joyce Cary described in his novel, *To Be A Pilgrim*: 'I feel the very presence of God, not only within me, but in the whole surrounding air, as love, friendship, beauty, so that it is as if these feelings existed not only within me but in the nature of things; as if the mountain, the clear sky, the little fields below, my friends, were bound together not by my feelings about them but by a reciprocal character of delight and understanding. I think I know what it means to have perfect faith; and as I turn again to climb I perceive that I belong to God.'

It is by repeating the mantra and keeping our eyes open that we become more aware of being a part of all creation. The eternal is all around us. We are part of the eternal rhythm of the universe where season follows season, and birth and death and resurrection are part of that universal rhythm. Meditation is like a seashell. We have but to lift it to our ears and we shall hear the music of the sea. We have but to listen and become that music, as in the Neil Diamond song: I am the song, sing me! I am the tune, play me! In the prayer of meditation we become the music and Brother James becomes his own Air.

 17

At the Heart of the Lotus Flower

The devout Muslim will learn by heart and chant the Qu'ran in its original just as devout Buddhists will learn and chant their sacred scriptures – the sutras – while Christian monks and nuns chant the Psalms day in and day out. Slowly, over the years, the words begin to resonate within. In his Holy Rule St Benedict counsels his monks to practise *lectio divinae* which means taking a sentence or a short passage and immersing one's self in it at a subliminal level, rather than merely an intellectual or academic level. And so one takes a text such as: 'Thou, O Lord, art in the midst of us', and explores it word by word.

THOU. The Italian and French languages in particular still use the second person plural for addressing strangers or those in authority, and the second person singular for family and intimates. Thus the French will address one as 'vous' until such time as the relationship has developed into one of intimacy when the form 'tu' is then employed. Today in English, however, the word 'Thou' – the equivalent of 'vous' – is no longer considered politically correct. Since God, however, is beyond our finite comprehension, I have no desire to say, 'Hey, you, God!' The word 'Thou' conveys a greater sense of awe and wonder. Interestingly, it is then followed by the next word: O. This word-sound, which is the same in every language, is also one of the most evocative of words. I recall Robert Frost talking about this in his log cabin in Vermont, and pointing out how 'There is the long 'o' sound I make all night when I have tooth-ache, and then there is the sharp 'o' sound I make when someone treads on my toe!' And when the actor playing Othello has to enter crying, 'O! O! O! O!' he has to find a way of filling those sound-words with the emotion that Othello is feeling at that moment. What the word-sound 'O' is saying is that there are no words to express what I feel. And so here, faced with the ultimate mystery of God, there are no words to convey the sense of awe and wonder.

LORD. This word means not only one who is my master, my teacher, but also 'Lord of all creation'. As we contemplate the vastness of the universe and the Intelligence that lies behind it, one is filled with awe and that is increased by the next word: ART. God is not an individual, God simply IS, God is pure being, pure essence, pure intelligence, pure meaning. All mystics, of every religion, acknowledge the is-ness of creation, what David Bohm refers to as 'the Implicate Order' of all creation.

And now come the final words of this short sentence: IN THE MIDST OF US. That which we acknowledge as the Transcendent One, whom we may call God, Allah, Abba, Ram – 'a rose by any other name would smell as sweet' – is in the whole of creation. As Gerard Manley Hopkins expresses it, 'The world is charg'd with the grandeur of God'. But this Transcendent One, the Divine Lover and Beloved as Rumi calls him, is also in our midst in other ways. Jesus said, 'The Kingdom of Heaven is within you' for, as all mystics have taught, we do not have to seek God for He is already within each one of us. As the Chadoga Upanishad so movingly puts it, 'In the centre of the Castle of Brahma, our own body, there is a small shrine in the form of a lotus flower and within can be found a small space. We should find who dwells there and want to know him, for the whole universe is in him and he dwells within our heart.'

We should indeed seek to know and understand that inhabitant. It is our task to nourish and kindle this light so that, like a lighthouse, its radiance spreads through all creation. As Jesus said, as the Buddha said, 'You are the light of the world.'

18

Through the Labyrinth

People's dreaming patterns vary but most of us know what it is to enter another dimension when we sleep. By day our busyness keeps the unconscious largely at bay – except when we are sad or depressed. At night, however, we relinquish control when we fall asleep and another world opens up. We may dream entire sequences, like the unfolding of a film or a novel. We encounter people we do not know and yet they seem as real as any we might meet in the street. Who are these people and where have they come from? What is this world one enters?

Of course it is possible to be swamped by this world and it is this fear that underlies the arguments sometimes put forward by evangelical Christians that 'unless the mind is always in control, one will be possessed by demonic forces,' as one of them once put it to me when challenging me about meditation. The practice of meditation requires exactly the opposite: in that we should put the mind to one side, and cease listening to its endless chatter. In the practice of meditation, whether we are following the breath or the mantra, we are grasping Ariadne's thread in order to find our way through the labyrinth of the unconscious. The moment that we attempt to still the mind and to centre down, the unconscious rises up to distract us in every possible way but, holding fast to the thread of our meditation, we gently acknowledge the clamour of these many siren voices, while continuing to descend deeper into the centre of our being for, paradoxically, it is from the unconscious that strength, wisdom and insight will arise.

The most famous ball of thread belonged to Ariadne, the beautiful daughter of King Minos of Crete who fell in love with Theseus when he arrived from Athens as part of the tribute of youths and maidens sent to the great labyrinth at Knossus to be sacrificed to the Minotaur, the monster who inhabited the labyrinth. Theseus promises to marry Ariadne if she will help him kill the Minotaur and escape. She gives him a ball of thread which he pays out as he enters the labyrinth so that, having killed the Minotaur, he can find his way out.

In Martha Graham's dance work, *Errand into the Maze*, Graham on entering the labyrinth cannot at first face the Minotaur, she is too terrified. It is only when she dares to turn and look him full in the face, to confront the very thing she fears, that she overcomes her fear and, mounting the Minotaur, rides him triumphantly out of the labyrinth. Folklore teaches that if you stare a wild animal in the eyes it will not attack you, and this is the best way to encounter the wild animal within oneself. The Monster in mythology, as also in our dreams, represents an aspect of our *shadow* side, an aspect that we are often reluctant to acknowledge and yet it is only by doing so that we can then harness its energy. Thus Prospero in Shakespeare's *The Tempest* is able at the end of the play to say of the monster Caliban (whom he has previously castigated as 'a devil, a born devil') 'This thing of darkness I acknowledge as my own.' Significantly Caliban replies to this, 'I'll be wise hereafter and seek for grace.'

The practice of meditation is like the end of a golden string and if we can only hold onto it until the end we shall indeed emerge, each of us, from our labyrinth. If, however, we try to ignore the *shadow* side it will only become more dangerous. Sometimes at work we may feel threatened by another member of staff but we need to question why we feel threatened. There may indeed be good reason, but we need also to ask ourselves: is it because this person is more talented, more successful, than I? What is it that we resent in them? A very little reflection will often show that all too often it is something we lack in ourselves. How often we have heard someone say of another person, 'Oh, she is so lazy, or stubborn, or stuck up!' when it is obvious that these are projections. Our worst enemy therefore is often found in the end to be our best friend. As Jack Kornfield says, 'To meditate and pray is like throwing the doors and windows open: you can't plan for the breeze!'

In the Upanishads, the sacred scriptures of India, we find the idea that God is buried in us as in a cave. The heart, which is where the Upanishads locate the presence of Atman, the Supreme Being, is likened to a cave and the soul to a treasure hidden in the midst of the body. Similar images are found elsewhere such as that of a book hidden for a long time in a cave and then found, or God hiding himself in a pearl that is difficult to find, the 'pearl of great price'. And so, as we persevere in meditation, we will find ourselves entering a still, serene space that we recognise as a 'holy of holies'. Once we have experienced this place we will know that it is beyond time and space and is where our essential being is to be found. 'In the body there is a shrine. In that shrine there is a lotus. In that lotus is a little space. What is it that lives in that little space? The whole universe is in that little space because the Creator, the Source of all, is in the heart of each of us.' Those words were spoken by Father Bede Griffiths in his ashram in southern India. He also said, 'All over the world people are awakening to the eternal reality and opening themselves to the Divine. Human beings are not separated souls but part of a web of interlocking relationships, connecting people and things.'

In the Upanishads it is said that 'The thread must in all things be followed back to its source.' The thread (sutra) is described as linking this world to the other world and all beings. The thread is both *atman* (self) and *prana* (breath) and is linked to the central point in the cosmos, the sun. In his book, *Catching the Thread*, Llewellyn Vaughan-Lee writes, 'Spiritual life is a response to a call. This call is like a golden thread that we follow, guiding us deeper and deeper within, always pointing to the beyond. It does not belong to the mind but to the deepest core of our being.'

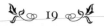

The Book of Books

In medieval times in the Judaic tradition a father would take his child to the rabbi to be taught to read. The rabbi would have a slate on which were written in chalk: the Hebrew alphabet, some sentences from the Torah, and the phrase 'May the Torah be your instruction'. The child would recite these aloud and when he had learned them by heart the rabbi would cover the slate with honey and the child would then eat the words. And so the words from the Book of Hosea 'When Thy words came I devoured them' may have a literal as well as a metaphorical meaning.

Many today, however, turn away from churches, synagogues and temples because there are often too many words. Living in a society that is inundated with words, words have often become meaningless through repetition, whether by clergy or politicians, so that words such as 'peace', 'justice', 'truth' are worn thin. Up and down the country in churches and chapels, Christians gabble the Lord's Prayer without pausing to reflect on the words. Words have become reduced to facts, mere information, and we have lost sight and sound of words as symbols. It is little wonder that so many long for a breathing space, for a silence that is as deep as the ocean. It is not that religions should not have their scriptures, their revealed teachings, but that words require space just as a plant requires light. The reason that Samuel Beckett wrote shorter and shorter plays was because he wanted to leave it to the actor to say more in the silences. I recall going to see John Hurt in Beckett's *Krapp's Last Tape*, a monologue, performed at the Barbican in London. Afterwards I remarked to him how potent were the long pauses and how we could sense what Krapp was thinking. 'I suddenly realised one day in rehearsal the point about Sam's work,' he replied, 'It is that his plays are one long silence occasionally interrupted by words!' There is a time for speaking and there is a time for not speaking; a time for words and a time for silence.

I have never forgotten buying a book by the Sufi master Idries Shah, entitled *The Book of Books*. I had already read a number of books on the Sufis and so, seeing this thick hard-backed volume in our local bookshop I added it to my collection. When I got home I began to read it at once. It tells the story of a wise man who taught his disciples from a seemingly inexhaustible store of wisdom. He attributed all his knowledge he said to a thick book which was kept in a place of honour in his room and which he would allow no one to open. After his death the book was handed down from one generation to another. It came to be known as the Book of Books. By now I had reached page eleven and it is at this point that Idries Shah tells the reader that in the pages that follow we shall find the content of the Book of Books.

There follow 260 pages of thick, white, and entirely blank paper! Each of those pages I 'read' slowly. I knew enough of Sufi teaching jokes to be aware that they are meant to be taken as seriously as any koan in Zen. I could easily have cheated, whipping through the pages, nodding sagely and saying, 'Yes, I get the point!' Instead I slowly turned page after blank page, absorbing the emptiness of each. The 'reading' of those pages remains for me to this day a rich and instructive experience. At the end I wrote on the final page some words from an early Buddhist text: 'The truth was never preached by the Buddha, seeing that you have to realise it within yourself.'

On the windowsill of my bedroom, in front of which I meditate, is a volume of the *Tao Te Ching*, the sayings of Lao Tzu. At intervals I learn a sentence or a verse by heart and then allow it to sink deep into myself. A few days ago I read the following: 'Forget knowledge, and you will remember all you need to know.' Sometimes, looking round the shelves of my library and especially at the section devoted to books on psychology, the history of religions, spirituality, biographies of mystics and other teachers, I wonder how much – or rather, how little – I have retained of them. So many millions of words. Theologians, above all, often write in such a complex and dense manner that the reader has to wrestle with the meaning even of a single sentence! When I think of the complexity of so much theology and then compare it with the simple, down-to-earth teaching stories of Jesus, as indeed of all true teachers, I cannot help recalling how the greatest theologian of all, St Thomas Aquinas, asked for his great work, *The Summa Theologica* to be burned because, in the light of a vision he had had, he realised how utterly inadequate it was.

I once was privileged to attend a *sama*, the meeting for worship by Muslim dervishes, at their centre in London. Just as I was opening my notebook to jot down impressions of their form of worship, Dr Rolls, the Sufi who had invited me, gently removed the book from my hands, indicating by her silent action that I should just be open to the experience. 'Forget knowledge, and you will remember all you need to know.' Later I was to learn what the twelfth-century philosopher and Sufi, El-Ghazali wrote: 'Onlookers whose motives are not worthy shall be excluded. The participants in audition must sit silently and not look at each other. They seek what may appear from their own hearts.' Words are labels, words are concepts, until they are made flesh. Only when we have learned to love may we speak of Love. Only when we have mastered our own warring elements may we speak of Peace. Without the experience the words remain concepts. The meaning of words goes deeper than the written words themselves. Every actor knows this. An actor may have to say the words 'I love you', but there is an infinite number of different ways of saying them and giving them meaning, according to the character and the situation. I remember Robert Frost , at the Bread Loaf Writers Conference in Vermont, remarking how 'Sometimes you think you know a poem by heart and then you hear an actor speak it, using a particular tone of voice on a word or a phrase, and suddenly it opens up a whole new dimension for you. An actor can cut your heart with these niceties.' We should, therefore, use words sparingly, letting them well up from the silence within. Rather than speak we should listen.

Once, celebrating a Eucharist at a church in London, because I had been rehearsing a new production all week and had had no time in which to prepare a homily, I placed a chair in front of the altar and when it came to the time to preach I sat in it, explaining that instead of a sermon we were all going to sit for the length of the usual homily, and listen to what the silence was trying to say to us. There is a time for words and there is a time for silence. And there is also a time to put away one's books. Here is a story to illustrate this. It is told by Shirley du Boulay in *The Cave of the Heart*, her award-winning biography of Swami Abhishiktananda (Father Henri le Saux), one of the most significant spiritual figures of the twentieth century. A Breton-born monk, he moved to India in 1948. It was his deep encounter with Hindu spirituality which led him to adopting the life of an Indian holy man, in the same way that Father Bede Griffiths, another Benedictine monk, also did, seeking to integrate the teachings of the Gospels with those of India's most sacred writings in the Upanishads. One of the ways in which Father Henri le Saux's openness to the Hindu experience was most remarkable was in his search for a teacher. Apart from the renowned Ramana Maharshi, who was to have such an influence on his life, there were several, but one in particular, Harilal Poonja, a Brahmin, and a disciple of Ramana Maharshi. He was a man who never minced his words. In one of his conversations Abhishiktananda (as he eventually came to be called) admitted that he liked quoting from the Bhagavad Gita and the Upanishads as he found it impressed people. He was about to quote a text, adding that he had learned a little Sanskrit, when Harilal interrupted him, saying, 'And what is the use of all that? All your books, all the time lost in learning different languages! Which language do you use to converse with the atman? The atman has nothing to do either with books, or with languages, or with any scripture whatever. It is – and that's all. It is only in the ultimate silence that the atman is revealed.'

 20

The Centre of the Dance

The 'whirling dervishes' form of worship, *sama*, is a sacred dance. It is a ritual in which the dance is sustained by a musical ensemble. The music itself is considered as a form of invocation, being an echo of the celestial music, aiming to awaken in the worshipper a desire to find once again the distant homeland from which we come and to which we return; for Islam, like Christianity, believes that we come from God and we return to God. The dance itself, in the form that was evolved by Rumi, and which he transmitted to his disciples, draws its efficacy from a rich and eloquent symbolism.

At the start the dervishes arrange themselves in concentric orbits, creating an image of the planets in the heavens. One dervish stands in the centre, representing the 'pole' of the universe, and begins to turn, at which the others all begin to turn in their individual orbits. At the start each has his hands crossed over his chest in a gesture of humility but, as they begin to spin, their arms spread out, the right hand open to the heavens, indicating that the worshipper is opening himself to the grace of heaven, and the left hand towards the ground, returning the grace to the world. Through his turning the dervish affirms the unique presence of God in all directions. As Sufis say: 'Wherever you turn there is the face of God.' Watching them I was most aware of their withdrawing to a spiritual centre, their faces becoming radiant from the intensity of their concentration, like the faces of lovers – indeed, all Sufis see themselves as the lovers of the Beloved. Watching them I thought of a passage from Plotinus:

> We are like a company of singing dancers
> Who may turn their gaze outward and away –
> Notwithstanding they have the choirmaster for centre;
> But when they are turned inwards towards him then they sing
>   true
> And are truly centred upon him
> Even so we encircle the Supreme always;
> But our eyes are not at all times fixed upon the centre.
> Yet in the vision thereof lie our attainment and our repose
> And the end of all discord:
> God in his dancers and God the true centre of the dance.

Today in the West we have lost touch with our bodies as a means of worship. Only Islam which requires five prostrations a day, and Tibetan Buddhism with its practice of many thousands of prostrations, and Yoga when used as a spiritual practice, understand the importance of involving our bodies in worship. I think that this was in part what attracted me to the history of the Shakers and led me first to write a radio documentary for the BBC, entitled *The Female Messiah*, and then to lead workshops exploring the rich tradition of Shaker dances, rituals, songs and hymns. Founded by Ann Lee from Manchester, a break away from the Quakers, the Shakers took root in America and became an important part of that country's heritage. Their ecstatic meetings would last for hours, breaking the barriers of fatigue and time and, rather in the manner of Gurdjieff's famous dances, releasing new energies. Their meetings would usually commence with everyone walking swiftly across the floor of the meeting house, each worshipper following a different path, each intent upon their individual journey, criss-crossing one another but never colliding: 'swiftly passing and re-passing each other like clouds agitated by a mighty wind'. This pattern would then be succeeded by a new one which consisted of each person, as they passed another, giving that individual a shove in the chest which would set them spinning, until eventually the whole assembly would be spinning like tops: 'reel, reel, reel into freedom! Shake out all the starch and stiff'ning!' Thereafter the movement would break up into a variety of patterns: jumping, rolling, tumbling, and so on, interspersed with songs or speaking in tongues.

At the end of one workshop, one of the participants, Cynthia O'Brien, who worked as a physiotherapist in a hospice, spoke at length about what she had learned from this experience of being shoved and so being precipitated into the whirling movement, similar to that of the dervishes. Normally in every day life, she said, if someone shoves us our response will be to hit back. In the Shaker ritual, however, you do not resist but you go with the movement, allowing it to send you into a spin. In yielding to this thrust the body is led into a whole sequence of movements, each flowing out from the other. It is all very Zen-like, reminiscent of the teachings of Lao Tzu who describes how when water, whether in a stream or a river, encounters an obstacle such as a rock, instead of hurling itself against it, flows round it, dividing itself in two and then continuing on the other side with renewed strength, having first absorbed the obstacle. This movement of push and yield is

central to the Shaker philosophy as best expressed in the words
of their hymn, *Simple Gifts*:

'Tis the gift to be simple,
'Tis the gift to be free.
'Tis the gift to come down
Where we ought to be.

And when we come round right
In the place just right
'Twill be in the valley
Of love and delight.

To bow and to bend
We shan't be ashamed.
To turn, turn, will be our delight
Till by turning, turning,
We come round right.

What Cynthia O'Brien, in her work with the dying, had
observed was how those who had the most difficult deaths
were always those people who had found it difficult in life to
yield, to let go, while those who died serenely tended to be
those who had learned how to be flexible, and

… to go with the drift of things,
To yield with a grace to reason,
To accept the end of a love or a season.
(Robert Frost)

A true ritual will always take one beyond and deeper than
words, for words are but symbols of a deeper reality. And so,
when we meditate, our posture, our way of sitting, of holding
ourselves erect and alert, will condition the quality of our
meditating, uniting body, mind and spirit.

Ed Hussein, in his memoir *The Islamist*, describing how he rediscovered his faith in Sufism, writes, 'Now, to bow and prostrate myself in prayer had meaning for me; abject humility, total lack of vanity, in following the Prophet Mohammed's motions of prayer before the unseen but all-seeing God.' The Prophet taught that one is closest to God in prostration, when the forehead, the bearer of intellect, is bowed in recognition of a higher knowledge, a celestial realm. 'In such a posture,' adds Ed Hussein, 'I was able to unearth the inner harmony of life.'

 21

Listening to the Sub-text

Milarepa, the Tibetan sage, warns, 'The concentration of inward quiet induces lassitude.' This is one of the dangers on the way and in the Way: that of quietism, of becoming so passive that meditation can begin to have as persuasive a hold as any drug. This particular danger is, psychologically, the call of the womb, inviting us to regress, to become wholly passive. Both spiritually and psychologically it is a call that must be resisted as vigorously as did Ulysses resist the call of the Sirens, even though it meant his being strapped to the mast of his ship so that he could not respond. And among alien surroundings, among people to whom we may not immediately respond or even find antipathetic, it is dangerously easy to withdraw into this inward quiet. Some even use it as a conscious technique in difficult encounters, hoping thereby to discourage others, or using it as a way of avoiding painful but necessary confrontation. All such temptations must be vigorously resisted. When we are alone we may withdraw but when we are in company with others we must always be present to them – albeit with a stillness at the centre – always ready to respond to the needs of others.

Meditation, as the Dalai Lama has said, should result in a greater awareness of others and of their needs, with a quickness to respond before even a word is said; ready to stand alongside someone even though we may have no words of wisdom to utter, just being present is what counts. As Jesus says to his friends in the Garden of Gethsemane, when he most needed them, 'Could you not watch with me one hour?' Only in this way will the person who meditates find the world in his heart. 'Meditation and the pursuit of wisdom,' says the Dalai Lama, 'should always issue forth in acts of compassion for others.' Or as Shantideva, the eighth-century Buddhist scholar, taught: 'May I be a boat, a bridge, a passage for those desiring the other shore.'

Even in the midst of much activity we can be listening inwardly. How many of us actually pause at intervals throughout the day in order to rest, if only for a moment, in the eternal silence, in the Now? Do we take time to reflect upon the pattern of the day's events and encounters? Do we listen for the sub-text of what people are really trying to say? Sometimes when someone telephones us and is chattering away, all we have to go on, if we are truly listening, is a tone of voice that alerts us to a deeper need behind their telephone call.

The more we listen to the silence, the more we shall begin to hear the silence in other people. The motto of the Dominican Order is: *Contemplare et contemplata tradere ad aliis*: to contemplate and to pass on to others the fruit of one's contemplation, or meditation. If we reflect on the life of Jesus we observe how the movement is continually between his absenting himself to a lonely place to pray, and being in the midst of the crowds: in the market place, in the temple, accessible, always at hand. We receive in order to give back, and we can see this in our own times in the life of Mother Teresa of Calcutta and many more.

In any book about meditation it is all too easy to become lop-sided, as though one is saying, 'Meditate and all shall be well.' However, we are creatures of body, emotions, intelligence, imagination, soul. The heart has its reasons but the body also has its own wisdom. If we neglect our bodies, do not feed or exercise or rest them properly, they will become subject to illness. And so when we are meditating it is important not to try and shut out an awareness of our bodies. As we sit we should be quietly aware of our feet firmly on the ground, the spine erect ('forwards and upwards' as the Alexander Technique teaches) and the arms and hands relaxed. Too much concentration upon the life of the spirit, especially in a beginner, can cause various kinds of mental and spiritual indigestion. We need to nourish our whole being. And just as it is said that we are what we eat, so similarly we are what we watch and read and listen to. We should read reflectively, allowing one book to lead us on to the next in an organic way; so too with music and art. The books we read, the music we listen to, the jobs we choose to do, the people we encounter, all go to the making of our story, of our song. 'Select, select!' writes Edwin Muir in a poem. 'Make an anthology of what's been given you by bold casual time. Revise, omit, keep what's significant.' Each of us has different experiences and encounters, each of us is on a different journey, yet the goal is the same. Some, as part of their search for wholeness, will explore the Alexander Technique, Shiatsu, Tai Chi, or some form of analysis or therapy. Some will have a strong need to express themselves through movement and dance, through painting, sculpture or some other form of creativity such as gardening, cooking: all these are creative ways of uniting body, mind, heart and spirit. Tasks can either be grudging chores or they can be redeemed by love, by our learning to be wholly in the present moment, as Buddhism teaches, whether it is washing up after a meal, or shopping in the supermarket. The more we allow ourselves to be in touch with our own centre, the less hurried we shall be, and the more open to each moment as well as to one another. Nothing is an end in itself but only a means to one true end in which our lives are made meaningful. The more we allow this process to unfold the more it will flow into our meditation and out again into our relationships with those around us, expressing itself in various forms of social commitment. The inner life is not a self-enclosed garden created only for our own delight. Once we have found the way to the centre our lives will become an open garden.

We have to work at ourselves, at our loves, at our relationships, at our work. Neglect at any level results in an imbalance and can lead to psycho-somatic illness or even psychic disorder. In society today, even in the 'alternative world', we pay lip service to certain ideals and concepts. We tend to act a role rather than be our authentic selves, perhaps because we don't fully know ourselves? In one of her last letters shortly before she died, Kathleen Mansfield wrote, 'I want to be what I am becoming.' To do this we have to give ourselves to the present moment.

 22

And in the Garden Secretly

I count myself fortunate, strange though it may sound, that in my early seventies I had cancer of the thyroid. I was entirely on my own at the time, as my partner was away in India. The fear was almost suffocating and yet I was glad to be alone to deal with it. It was then that I learned, as Holderlin expresses it, that 'where danger is, grows also the rescuing power.' One night, at the peak of my fear, I awoke to hear an interior voice saying, 'You are not alone. You have an angel working alongside you.' From that moment the fear began to subside so that when I went in for the four-hour operation, not knowing whether I would be able to speak when I came out of it, for the vocal organs are perilously close to the thyroid, I was entirely without fear. Who is to explain the origin of that voice? It is possible that it came from the unconscious, that repository of wisdom that lies beyond the intellect; but I do not discount, any more than does the biologist Rupert Sheldrake, that there may be angelic powers. In the Celtic tradition there is a strong sense that each of us has an invisible companion who walks the road of life with us, and one of the poverties of modern life is the loss of belief in such presences. The late John O'Donohue, in *Eternal Echoes*, wrote of the Christian tradition which says that when we are sent here on earth a special angel is chosen to accompany our every step, breath, thought and feeling. 'This is your guardian angel, who is right beside you, as near as your skin. You are not on your own. If you could see your path with the eyes of your soul, you would find that it is a luminous path and that there are two of you walking together. You are not alone. When loneliness or helplessness overcomes you, it is time to call on your angel for help and courage.' It was only long after that I came across his book and when I reflected on the whole experience, I was moved to find those same words: You are not alone.

It is in the Garden of Gethsemane that Jesus confronts his own fear and is comforted by an angel. If we spend our lives seeking a way back to that Garden in which man and woman lived in harmony with the Divine, it has to be by way of the Garden of Gethsemane and the Garden of the Tomb. A garden is a place for cultivation where one has to weed, dig, plant, prune, and all gardens are, in one way or another, an unconscious attempt to recreate that first garden in Eden. In a garden we encounter both death and resurrection. This is why the story of the Gardens is an archetypal one that affects us all at the deepest level. In the Garden of Gethsemane Jesus is deserted by his closest friends who fall asleep ('Could you not watch *one* hour with me?'), betrayed by Judas, tortured, and put to death, dying with the final cry of 'My God, *why* have you forsaken me?'

And then three days later something unexpected happens, however we explain it. Early on the Sabbath, while it is still dark, Mary who loved Jesus so deeply that Judas was shocked by the excess of her love, comes to the tomb and is distressed to find it empty, and the body of Jesus gone. 'They have taken away my Lord and I know not where to find him.' She is overwhelmed, as we so often are, by grief, anger, bitterness, engulfing us so that we can no longer see who is standing right in front of us.

'The meaning has gone out of our lives!' we cry. 'There is no sense any more. We are lost, and the one person, the one love, who did make sense of it all has been cruelly snatched away, even his body, even the memory of his love!'

And then very quietly the voice speaks to us.

'Why are you weeping?'

And we reply to that voice, not even recognising it, 'Because my life is empty! And I no longer know where my love, my life, my Lord is!'

Then it is, in that hushed garden, as dawn is breaking, the sun inching up over the hills, and the first birds singing, that the voice speaks our name, so softly in the stillness, saying, Mary! James! Hywel! Celia! That voice speaks our name as no one else will ever speak it or can say it, and we know then that we are recognised. He whom we thought we had lost has found us and he knows us as we truly are, what we are capable of and what we can be. He sees us in the fullness of our being, as we yearn to be and stumble to become. And like Mary we cry out to the Divine Beloved with joy, reaching our arms to enfold him, saying, 'Master! Friend! Beloved! Teacher!'

In life there are very few who love us in the totality of our being, even among supposedly good friends. Most people love us for themselves because we mirror them, gratify or complement them. When we fail to measure up to their expectations they cast us away, reject or even savage us in their disappointment. It is never so with the Divine Lover. He embraces us all, as do our true friends, in our weakness, our vanity, our unbelief, from Peter to Thomas to Mary. He embraces each one of us.

So here is a meditation with a difference, for a special occasion, perhaps when we are especially troubled or desolate, unable to see beyond our pain. If the place where we live is crowded or noisy then let us go for a walk and find somewhere quiet where we can sit with closed eyes. Seated there, in a city square or a park or field, we imagine the garden of our dreams: it may be a particular garden of our childhood, or one we have known or visited, or it may be a garden of our imagining. It may be a garden like King Arthur's island valley of Avilion in Tennyson's *The Passing of Arthur*:

> Where falls not hail or rain, or any snow
> Nor ever wind blows loudly, but it lies
> Deep-meadowed, happy, fair, with orchard lawns
> And bowery hollows crowned with summer seas,
> Where I will heal me of my grievous wound.

In our imagination we see the garden very clearly, we walk in it, discover its trees, flowers, rocks, water; we listen to the secret sounds of the garden, until it is all there in our mind's eye. And then, still with eyes closed, we find a sheltered spot in our imagined garden where we can sit and wait for our Beloved to come. In the hush of dawn, or the quiet of dusk, we sit and wait, knowing that when he speaks he will call us by our name.

The message of the eternal garden, of the garden that was in Eden, the garden that was at Gethsemane, and the garden of the Tomb, is that of love. Love is the key that will unlock the secret garden within each one of us. Love sharpens the perceptions, fuses the vision. We only live truly, we only live fully, when we love truly, love fully; when we are in the Divine Beloved and He is in us, beyond all clutter of dogma and of rules. To love is to live. It is the only way of living. It is no wonder, therefore, that Mary ran from the garden, saying 'I have seen the Lord!'

 23

Alone with the Wild Beasts

At the age of thirty Jesus goes to be baptised by his cousin and contemporary, John, in the River Jordan. As he comes up out of the water he receives an interior confirmation of what his vocation is, for which he has been preparing since birth. He then goes into the desert for forty days where, we read, 'he was alone with the wild beasts and angels ministered unto him.' There may well have been wild animals in the desert but it seems as likely that, before launching on his life's work, he had finally to deal with his own inner wild beasts. Going into retreat is essential at key moments in one's life. I recall how in my thirties I would go away for two or three days to somewhere unfamiliar in order to be entirely on my own. By day I would take long walks and talk to myself. But it was in the nights that my own wild beasts would emerge, when I would have to face hidden angers, resentments, fears, lusts, jealousies. Always, however, by confronting them, I would experience healing and growth. As Carl Jung wrote: 'The highest and most decisive experience of all is to be alone with one's own self. The individual must be alone if he is to find out what it is that supports him when he can no longer support himself. Only this experience can give him an indestructible foundation.'

In *The Christian Archetype*, a Jungian comment on the life of Christ, Edward F. Edinger, in a chapter on the Agony in the Garden, writes: 'The source of inner strength constellated by prayer or active imagination is personified in St Luke's Gospel by the ministering angel.' There will be times when our half hour – or longer of meditation will seem unendurable, when we are assailed by thoughts and feelings, resentments and lusts, as by a swarm of angry bees in August deprived of their honey. Yet we learn to hang on like a mountaineer climbing a particularly steep cliff face. It may only be in the final moments of the meditation that we experience the stillness and, as it were, the presence of angels.

The practice of meditation is an ongoing discipline but there will always be up days and down days. Some days we will find ourselves slipping easily into the stillness of meditation as into a river, and then there will be other days when we seem unable to swim and are struggling against the tide. Through our practice, however, we learn patience and endurance, as well as the wisdom of waiting, knowing that there is a time and a season for everything under the sun.

A Sioux Prayer:

> I seek strength, not to be greater than my brother,
> But to fight my greatest enemy – myself.

24

Doors Opening and Closing

I once dreamed that I was moving in a landscape of tall doors
in a vast space as high as the sky. They were not doors in the
accepted sense. They had no top, there were no handles. They
had no other delineation than formal steps ascending to each.
They were doors carved out of rock, massive and immovable.
How could I ever hope to open one? To what realms did these
doors lead? How to enter them all? 'They are the doors of
many possibilities,' said a voice. 'But only one or two will open
for you. If you are patient then the intended opportunity will
appear.' Footsteps echoed. The only other sound was that of
many sighs. They were the sighs of those who did not wait and
so missed their opportunity. They were the sighs of those who
knew that they could never pass this way again.

Sometimes in life we find that the door which we are
convinced is ours will not open or, if opened, leads only to an
empty space; or else we find that one room leads to another,
door after door, until we are hopelessly lost. Sometimes
we hear lilting music, laughter and voices from behind a
particular door and we long to enter. Perhaps we even force
our way in only to be thrown out, hearing the door close
behind us with a resounding and final bang. At other doors
we knock and knock, bruising our knuckles, until we finally
give up in despair.

The poet John Keats understood about doors. In 1818, while
staying in Teignmouth, he wrote to a friend, 'I will put down
the simile of human life as far as I now perceive it. I compare
human life to a large mansion of many apartments, two of
which I can only describe, the doors of the rest being as yet
shut upon me. The first we step into we call the Infant or

Thoughtless Chamber, in which we remain as long as we do not think. We remain there a long while and notwithstanding the doors of the second chamber remain wide open, showing a bright appearance, we care not to hasten to it; but are at length imperceptibly impelled by the awakening of the Thinking principle within us. We no sooner get into the second chamber which I shall call the Chamber of Maiden Thought, than we become intoxicated with the light and the atmosphere, we see nothing but pleasant wonders, and think of delaying there for ever in delight. However, among the effects this breathing is father of, is that tremendous one of sharpening one's vision into the heart and nature of Man, of convincing one's nerves that the world is full of Misery and Heartbreak, Pain, Sickness, and Oppression, whereby this chamber of Maiden Thought becomes gradually darkened, and at the same time – on all sides of it – many doors are set open – but all dark – all leading to dark passages – we see not the balance of good and evil, we are in a mist – *we* are now in that state, we feel 'the burden of the mystery'.

Jesus said, 'Seek and ye shall find; knock and it will be opened unto you'. But many will say, 'What mockery is this? How can He say, "Knock and it will be opened unto you"? when in every part of the world so many have been disappointed, betrayed, broken, crippled, destroyed. No doors have opened for them, and in the night time they cry out on their lonely beds, "My God, My God, why have you forsaken me!"'

For the disciples after Calvary it was as though a door had slammed in their faces. They, too, were broken, disillusioned, downcast. Three days later Easter morning was to change all that. What I find strange is that in spite of the belief in resurrection so many Christians remain afraid of death, unlike Hindus and Buddhists who know how to prepare for dying. In part it is because too little is taught in our society about dying and death, and also because we use the noun 'death' and the adjective 'dead' with their harsh and final sounds as of a prison door closing upon us. Yet death is but a transition, as Swedenborg taught; death is not extinction, but simply the transition from one state to another. We pass through a door from one space to another. We die but to be reborn. And exactly how we go through that final door, how we die, will depend upon how we respond to the many hourly, daily, yearly experiences of dying we encounter in our lives: how we respond to the dying of a hope, a dream, a friendship, an ambition, a passion. If we learn how to live through each of these miniature deaths then each will become a resurrection, every ending a new beginning. If on our journey down the years we do this then we shall also hear, increasingly nearer, that music from another room which is the life that is beyond and yet, at the same time, is all about us even now. And if continually, hourly, daily, yearly, we learn how to die and be reborn then we shall find that after long searching a door does open and there is a way ahead when we had thought no door would ever open to us. It may not be the door we expected, nor the door we would have chosen for ourselves, but it has opened and we have but to enter.

Each of us has to learn how to wait in order for our door to open. Too often we are seeking the wrong door and, like Emily Dickinson, we find ourselves 'looking oppositely for the Kingdom of Heaven'. One door closes and another opens. The truth is that the door which is most uniquely ours has been there all the time, only we could not see it. Although a few seem to know from the start where they are going, most of us have to learn to wait for our door to reveal itself. When the door opens we can have little warning as to what form it will take. It might be, as it was for Karol Wojtyla, a lofty and mighty door of resounding bronze opening upon the awesome responsibility of being Pope, or it may be a door so small that we have to go down on our hands and knees if we are to enter it. And so after all it is true: Seek and ye shall find. Whether we are Christians, Muslims, Hindus, Sikhs, Jews, we have but

to seek God and we have already found him. There are many
doors and yet in the end there is but one Door. To each and
every one of us the Divine Lover and Beloved says:

I am the Way – walk me!
I am the Truth – sing me!
I am the Life – live me!

On Rejection and Betrayal

In a recent article in *The Sunday Times* Olivia James described
how two months after having given birth to their second
child her husband left her for another woman. 'We had been
together for fourteen years. He was my first love; I was his.
He had been my life, my home. I thought I was his.' The pain
of such rejection and betrayal is all too common. Similarly
in a work situation a colleague, or our boss, whom we have
trusted and appeared to get on well with, can suddenly turn on
us. We are misrepresented, slandered, stabbed in the back, left
with a deep sense of injustice, and dreams of revenge. Alone
in the small hours of the morning we lie awake, tormented
by the pain of such betrayal, which may have resulted in
our being demoted, passed over, or even thrown out of our
job. Sometimes when pupils unfairly accuse a teacher of
abuse, the teacher is removed from his or her job, pending
police investigations which can drag on for months. In every
instance we feel devalued, cast out, made a scapegoat even. We
can either choose to nurse a grievance, refuse ever to see that
person again, or go anywhere near the place that once was so

familiar to us. Many indeed nurse grievances for long years, refusing to let go of the pain which then only eats into them the more.

As failures, bitternesses, betrayals, woundings and our own obstinacies well up, we have to learn how to deal with them then and there. If we repress and suppress them they will only redouble their attacks. And so we have to confront them, look them in the face like the dreaded Minotaur – but not during our meditation time, even though predictably they will almost inevitably arise to distract us. If the woundings of betrayal or loss go very deep they will almost inevitably flare up during our meditation. Each time the pain or anger arises we must face it head on, acknowledge it while breathing in the pain, and then, on the outgoing breath, let it go. And we continue like this, breathing in the pain and releasing it, before returning to focus on the breath or on the mantra. We rest in the darkness, in the emptiness, and slowly, over hours, weeks, months, something mysterious begins to happen. Gently, barely discernible, our psyches are purified as in the silence of meditation psychological knots are loosened, and those secret poisons which invade our psyches are slowly drained away. It is not a process that can be hurried.

We cannot escape suffering in one form or another, whether physical or mental. It is part of the human condition. But when it does come then it presents us with a challenge. We can either resent, resist it, or we can regard it as an opportunity for growth. All the time, though we often cannot see this, pain in whatever form erodes more of our ego, as we are being slowly shaped to our true end. Often rejection or betrayal reveal aspects of ourselves that we don't want to acknowledge. It may be in fact that we are insensitive to other people's feelings or are too forceful in our dealings with them, and this is why they have turned on us. It may be that we interfere too much in other people's lives or work, thinking we know better. At other times, of course, the problem lies not within us but in the other person who is projecting onto us their own shadow side. Reflecting on all this we can at least begin to understand the other person and how the situation has arisen, even if it does not immediately resolve the problem.

We have to learn how to distinguish the situation, the argument, from the person. If we don't, we will simply turn the other person into our enemy, projecting onto them all our pain. When the pain of rejection or betrayal is very intense, as I have known it, it can be helpful to have a mantra that we can repeat, holding onto it like a lifeline, in order to gently detach ourselves from the murderous, vengeful thoughts that assail us: those melodramas in which we imagine ourselves saying 'I will never see that person ever again, or speak to them!'

Revenge is never sweet for it never satisfies. Even if we were to murder the other person, the pain would not be buried with them for a deeper guilt would remain. We have to let go even of dreams of revenge, and all murderous thoughts. One mantra that I have found helpful is from Shakespeare's *The Winter's Tale*. When the queen, Hermione, is unjustly sent to prison by her jealous husband Leontes, she says 'This action that I go on is for my better grace.'

It is also worth remembering that rejection and betrayal lie at the heart of the Christian story. Judas, one of the Twelve, betrays Jesus, while Peter denies that he knows Jesus. Peter's rejection stems from fear of being associated with Jesus who has been arrested, but Judas' act of betrayal is more complex. He represents the *shadow* side of that small group. In every group there is likely to be found someone who is carrying the group projection and will either be made the scapegoat or more actively betray the group. Until we have learned to be aware of the *shadow* side of our psyches we shall continue to be taken by surprise. As Anthony Stevens writes in *Private Myths*: 'At the core of the *shadow* complex is the archetype of the Enemy. Learning to live on good terms with "the enemy within" means that one is less likely to project it onto other people and, as a result, one makes one's own contribution to peace and understanding in the world.'

Recognising parts of the Self as personifications of complexes such as the *shadow*, the *animus*, the *anima*, the *father*, *mother*, *child*, making them conscious, and relating to them as one would to real personalities, creates not only greater strength and harmony within, but improves one's capacity to interact with other people in the outer world as well. It is clear that this is exactly what Jesus was doing in the desert when he was alone with the wild beasts and the Devil.

Jung comments on how the story of the Temptation clearly reveals the nature of the psychic power with which Jesus came into collision: it was the power-intoxicated devil of the prevailing Caesarean psychology that led him into dire temptation in the wilderness. This devil, says Jung, was the objective psyche that held all the peoples of the Roman Empire under its sway, and that is why it promised Jesus all the kingdoms of the earth, as if it were trying to make a Caesar of him. Obeying the inner call of his vocation, Jesus voluntarily exposed himself to the assaults of the imperialistic madness that filled everyone, conqueror and conquered alike. In this way he recognised the nature of the objective psyche which had plunged the whole world into misery and had begotten a yearning for salvation that found expression even in the pagan poets. 'Far from suppressing or allowing himself to be suppressed by this psychic onslaught, Jesus let it act on him consciously, and assimilated it. Thus the world-conquering Caesarism transformed into spiritual kingship, and the Roman Empire into the universal kingdom of God that was not of this world.'

Snakes and Ladders

We should not be distressed by lapses from grace. They may well be necessary. We may have been trying too hard and so need to let up for a while. Or we may have become too inflated by what we imagine as our progress in meditation so that a sudden fall from grace jerks us back to earth. It is like the game of Snakes and Ladders. Meditation is an ever-renewed game as time and again we slide to the bottom of the ladder. Of course if we concentrate on winning – whatever that might mean – the game will seem even more pointless and more frustrating. We do not play to win, not in the game of meditation.

Once a year perhaps, in the game of Solitaire, all the marbles disappear until only one is left in the centre. And we gaze at the circular board and the single marble and rest content. It is what Zen masters call a moment of *satori*: a sense of having broken through, of union with That Which is Desired, when everything seems to fall into place. It is often after such an experience that we fall most lamentably from grace. 'It had been a splendid day', wrote T.H. White in *The Goshawk*. 'He would go back. He was sure to. Goshawks, and this was the second time I had learned from experience, went back two paces every time they went forward one. "There is no short cut" said the good book, my manual, "to the training of the goshawk."'

Listening to the Voice
of the Wind

In the *Duino Elegies* Rilke writes: 'But listen to the voice of
the wind, and the ceaseless message that forms itself out of
the silence.' In the practice of silent meditation we learn to set
aside the clamour of the many voices of the ego, as well as what
Eckhart Tolle refers to as 'the pain body' with its ceaseless cries
of Me! Me! Me! We simply sit, waiting and listening. In some
ways meditating is like planting a bulb. We water it but we can't
see anything happening. We have to have faith that there in the
darkness, underground, it will begin to put down roots as well
as to push upwards towards the light. So it is with the practice
of meditation: we are as the earth, holding and protecting the
seed in deep darkness.

Peter Craig-Wild, an Anglican priest, in the autumn of
2002, spent a sabbatical with the Cherokee Indians in America.
He found them to be a quiet people with a deep inner
stillness. He asked one of the elders how white people could
begin to learn from them. His reply was that they should go
and sit in the forest for a day and listen to it. The Cherokees,
he said, would often sit out of doors and gaze at a rock, a
lake, or a mountain top. There, he said, they would meet with
God. 'God speaks to us rather than we speak to God.' One has
only to contrast this with the average service in a Christian
church with its endless readings, admonitions, sermon and
many prayers. Where, one asks, is the silence in which we can
listen to God?

Spirituality has to do with the inner depths of a person and
it is when we learn to listen inwardly and attentively to the

claims of the spirit that renewal comes. The words 'Be still and know that I am God' speak of an existential experience of something Other – which some may call God, or Allah, or Atman. Learning to listen inwardly also makes us more alert to those messages that come to us from time to time in dreams. It is as though through such dreams the wisdom of the unconscious is trying to reach us.

In walking through an overgrown wood one is often torn by brambles, tripping over roots, having to duck under branches and, because often there are no paths, losing our way. Then we come to a clearing in the woods and there is a sudden calm. The sky is overhead, a lark is singing high up, and we can pause to take stock before continuing our journey.

 28

Into Great Silence

Following the breath as it flows in we pause for a moment upon completion of the breath before allowing it to flow out. When all the breath is expelled we rest in the emptiness, until the breath begins once again to flow back in. We do not try to control the breath: this is not a keep-fit breathing exercise! We simply allow the breath to find its own rhythm and the more centred we become we shall find the breaths becoming shallower, almost imperceptible at times. As we allow the breath to flow in and to flow out we need to become more aware of the silence and the space that surrounds each breath, for in meditation we are listening intently to that silence which surrounds us. We need to learn how to listen to the silence behind the silence, even to what the silence may be trying to tell us. 'Be still and know that I am God': but this kind of knowing is not of the mind, but of the heart. It is a felt knowledge, intuitive rather than intellectual.

Breathing in and breathing out we begin to see that we are surrounded and upheld by this silence. It is a little like floating in the sea on one's back. If we didn't breathe we would sink, so the breathing is essential but as we gently breathe in and out so we float upon the deep waters and gaze up into the infinity of the sky above.

However, for those who are by nature doctrinaire and who require certainties, such profound silence and peace can be frightening. Yet as Thomas Merton discovered when he visited the famous Cave of the Buddhas at Polonnaruwa in Kandy and was profoundly moved by the silence of those extraordinary faces, it is in such profound silence that all problems are resolved and everything is made clear. As he wrote in his diary, 'Everything is emptiness and everything is compassion.'

There is a three-and-a-half-hour film, *Into Great Silence*, which depicts the life of the Carthusian monks at the famous Monastery of La Trappe in the Alps, and is shot mainly in silence. The title implies that while there is silence which is simply the absence of sound, there is beyond it a greater silence which is an intimation of, an experience of, timelessness, of the eternal in the present. And the more we learn in meditation to listen to this silence the more we come to realise that it is our natural element, the source of all energy and life, in which we live and move and have our being.

29

The Pattern in the Rug

A blank page, a blank canvas, a block of stone. The writer or composer, painter, sculptor, all wait for something: an inspiration. While waiting, however, each continues daily to work at their craft, whether or not he or she feels like it. I remember the painter Keith Vaughan telling me how always he had to be in his studio each morning at the same time, and work for the same number of hours, whether or not he felt like it. It is the same with the practice of meditation.

Robert Frost used to tell how he came to write what is perhaps his most celebrated lyric, *Stopping By Woods On A Snowy Evening*. He had been up all night in his log cabin in Vermont, working at a long piece of blank verse which wasn't going anywhere. Then at dawn he put down his pen and stood at the window to watch the sun rise. At that moment there came into his head, in its entirety, the poem *Stopping By Woods*, and all he had to do was to write it down. 'That,' he said, 'is what you might call the luck of the work. Yet it might never have happened had I not been labouring all night over that other piece of work.' The artist knows that underneath, in the unconscious, seeds are stirring. Then the day comes that a new work is created. And we also one day look up from our meditating and are aware that, quite suddenly, we have moved on. Certain problems have fallen away from us, certain attitudes or prejudices have shifted and changed. A new awareness is born. And so in meditation we continue with our practice, in season and out of season, just as in a committed relationship we remain constant in sickness and in health, for richer or poorer till death do us part. And then, like an artist, we may experience from time to time certain insights.

Coleman Barks, in *The Selected Poems of Rumi*, tells the following story. A man in prison is sent a prayer rug by a friend. What he had wanted, of course, was a file or a cross-bar or a key! But he began using the rug for performing the five prostrations and prayers before dawn, at noon, at mid-afternoon, after sunset, and before sleeping. Bowing, sitting up, bowing again, he notices an odd pattern in the weave of the rug, just at the point where his head touches. He studies and meditates on that pattern until he gradually realises that it is a diagram of the lock that confines him to his cell, and how it works. And so he is able to escape. 'Anything you do everyday,' concludes Coleman Barks, 'can open into the deepest spiritual place which is freedom.'

At The Threshold

I have a painting given to me by the artist Celia Read which is entitled 'At The Threshold'. It is an oblong of deep red in the centre of which is an opening like a doorway but in front of which is a screen of red, and all round it, as though seeping through from the other side, is a deeper, warmer pink. It is as though the screen is protecting one from the brilliance of light that lies beyond. In the foreground of the painting, low down, is a thick bar of black like a step in front of a door. When I wake in the night the picture is just a large oblong of blackness against the pale wall. Then in the early hours it starts to glow like the dawn itself and gradually I become aware of the screen and the light beyond, while the thick black line is like a sign saying, 'Halt! Go no further! Wait!' and so, at different hours of the day and the night I find myself meditating upon the theme 'At the threshold.'

I am also reminded of the account given to me by a friend who, while having an operation for a quadruple bypass, had a near-death experience. Her husband had died a few years before. Like everyone else who has had such an experience she saw herself rise up; she could see the two surgeons and the anaesthetist, then she began to float, as though she was swimming. Finally she upended herself and saw ahead of her a tall screen shielding her from a blazing brilliant light behind. Standing at the base of it was her husband, dressed not in his usual tweeds but in a golden robe. 'Henry!' she cried and began to run excitedly towards him, crying 'Hold me! Hold me!' but he replied, 'I cannot because I am not of your world.' Again she repeated her plea and then, – and at this point she said, words began to fail her – but as though from every side of him, although he did not touch her, a great warmth arose, enveloped and held her. It was, she said, golden – the only word she could find. Since then, she said, as does everyone who has had such an experience, 'I no longer have any fear of dying.'

Meditation is a natural technique which is not dependent upon any religious dogma but which, if persevered in, results in a more centred, balanced and aware sense of our being no longer at the mercy of the vicissitudes of events or emotions. And for many this is sufficient. It deepens our humanity as well as our compassion for others. But for some the practice of meditation may prove to be a threshold at which they have a sense of being in the presence of something greater than themselves. At such a moment there is a sense, as from behind a partially open door, of the sound of music from another room, a glimpse of a more intense life awaiting one. It is an experience of the Transcendent which we may, or may not, choose to call 'God'. The name, however, is less important than the experience which is inviting us to go further and deeper into the unknown.

John O'Donohue, in his final book, *The Lost Art of Blessing,* reminds us that originally the word 'threshold' related to the word 'thresh' which was the separation of the grain from the husk or straw when oats were flailed. It also includes the notions of 'entrance', 'crossing', 'border', and 'beginning'. To cross a threshold therefore is to leave behind the husks and arrive at the grain. As I grow older it seems to me increasingly that all one can do is to prostrate one's self at the Threshold of Mystery. It is there, at the threshold, that we sense something beyond dogma, beyond theology, for we are now moving beyond concepts, beyond words, into the Silence behind the silence where, like Shakespeare's Pericles we begin to hear 'the harmony of the spheres'. As Sufism teaches: we come from God and we are returning to God. It is at this Threshold that we glimpse the unutterable, the inexpressible, the unimaginable Beauty that lies ahead of us, but is also hidden deep within each one of us.

As the ancient Irish greeting says: 'May the stars light your way and may you find the interior path. Forward!'

Brother James' Air

A threshold is a place of coming and going. It is a frontier which challenges us to cross over or else go back. At a frontier we have to declare our identity. A frontier marks the division between one territory and another and so the journey to the frontier is often one from the known to the unknown. What lies on the other side may be desired: an El Dorado of our dreams, an Utopia; or it may be Hades, the Burning

Fiery Furnace, the Waste Land. Mythology and the history of religions are full of stories and rituals relating to the departure of a man's soul from the world and its journey to the distant land of spirits. Many tales are told of journeys across the River Styx to Hades: the descent of Orpheus to bring back Eurydice, of Dionysus to bring back Semele, and the voyage of Odysseus to the ends of the ocean. The daily descent of the sun beneath the frontier of the horizon led naturally to a belief that a Land of the Departed Souls lay in the Far West, in the world below. And if mortals could cross this frontier to the world beyond it was equally possible for spirits to cross over from the other side. A child looking into a mirror, as Alice found, has intimations of such possibilities.

Tennessee Williams' play *Camino Real* concerns the attempt by various characters to cross the frontier. The Land Beyond the Mountains we are told is known as Terra Incognita, the unknown land. In the play Marguerite, La Dame aux Camélias, says to her lover, Casanova, 'You don't really want to leave here. The truth of the matter is that you're terrified of the Terra Incognita outside that wall!' to which he replies, 'You've hit upon the truth. I am terrified of the unknown country inside or outside this wall or any place on earth without you with me.' Lord Byron, the poet, successfully escapes, saying 'It is time to leave here. There is a time for departure even when there's no certain place to go. Make voyages! Attempt them! There is nothing else.' However, when Marguerite attempts to leave on the plane called the Fugitivo, she discovers that there is no reservation in her name and that her papers are lost. Without her passport she has no identity, no means of moving on. Like Blanche du Bois in *A Streetcar Named Desire* she has reached the point of no return. Tennessee Williams' play is a moving image of so many today, especially the young, who are metaphorically without passports, without a true identity. They do not know who they are, where they have come from, or where they are going.

In his diary Dag Hammarskjold, the former General Secretary of the United Nations, often referred to 'the frontier of the unheard of'. Meditation is such a threshold, such a frontier. And in meditation, paradoxically, we ourselves are the frontier. As the breath comes in and goes out we become aware the deeper truth of those words 'I am the Way'.

Meditation is as natural as the air we breathe, and as necessary. The word 'air' means also a melody in music, as when we speak of *Brother James' Air*. Meditation, like prayer, is that harmony of the spheres to which Shakespeare so often refers. Meditation is like a sea-shell; we have but to place it to our ear and we hear the music. 'I am the song – sing me! I am the tune – play me!' are words from a song by Neil Diamond. In meditation we become that music: Brother James becomes his own air.

The state of being at the Threshold is one of watching, waiting and listening. We call out into the darkness, 'Who's there?' and a voice replies, 'I am that I am. I am the Way – walk me!' Throughout the long hours of the darkness each of us is a Guardian of the Threshold.

All myths concerning the frontier are maps of an interior reality. At the deepest level the frontier is within each one of us. And that frontier leads to other frontiers that we must cross as we search for the continuously unfolding mystery of life and its meaning. Only at the end of the journey may it be said of us as it was of Gilgamesh, 'He was wise, he saw mysteries, and knew secret things. He went on a long journey, was weary, worn out with labour, and returning, engraved on a stone the whole story.'

Sleeping Every Night
Beneath a New Sky

Each of us has a story to tell, one life to live, one song to sing and the deep fear in many is less that of physical death than that of dying with their story untold, their life unlived, their song unsung. Every human being, says Jung, has an unique story to tell, and no one can discover their greatest meaning unless they live out their own story. As Laurens van der Post wrote, 'One must be ready to obey the story and add one's mite to it. I might even say in hindsight that obedience to the private and most intimate summons of the imagination is to live symbolically and religiously.'

To obey one's story, to heed the inner images that well up, can be a painful process and yet, to quote Robert Frost again, 'we live by shedding'. The agony of breaking through personal limitations and going beyond them is the agony of spiritual growth. It is a process that all creative artists know. Art, literature, music, and myth, are instruments to help us past our limited and limiting horizons as we cross threshold after threshold. In the Sumerian *Epic of Gilgamesh* the hero searches for the answer to the meaning of life and death. At each frontier he is questioned afresh, 'For what reason have you made this great journey, crossing the seas whose passage is difficult? Tell me the reason for your coming.' And each time Gilgamesh answers, 'It is to see Utnapishtim whom we call the Faraway that I have come this journey. I wish to question him concerning the living and the dead, how shall I find the life for which I am searching?'

Spiritual growth means the growth of the whole psyche. No amount of praying, no amount of meditating, will enable us to grow spiritually unless our whole life is opened up to the influence of the Spirit. Those who are locked into their own opinions, self-importance or prejudice; those who are afraid to change, to give up, to let go; those who do not even begin to listen to others, who cannot entertain contrasting points of view or alternative lifestyles; those who persistently ignore the counsel of their dreams or of their bodies, all these are refusing to grow spiritually.

No amount of cutting weeds on a lawn will prevent the weeds spreading. Until the roots are dealt with the weeds will merely multiply. For several summers in Wales I observed countless small shoots all over the lawn which, however often they were mown, appeared to grow stronger. Finally I dug down and discovered that all across the lawn, like varicose veins, extended a network of tough, woody shoots, so that the lawn had to have incisions made all over it before the long sinewy roots could be ripped out. It takes courage to carry out such surgery, whether on a lawn or on one's self. Most people prefer to cling to their neuroses, their illnesses, their prejudices, and their established patterns of work and behaviour. Any suggestion of change threatens them for change means upheaval, and once you start more change will follow. Change is an uncomfortable business for it leads to unknown and unexpected adventures. It means letting go of our psychological and emotional possessions.

To be open to change is to be willing to go on a journey of the spirit, like Gilgamesh. At the end of *King Lear* Kent says, 'I have a journey yet to go', and in *The Four Quartets* T.S. Eliot reminds us, 'Old men should be explorers.' True spiritual growth means a willingness to travel. There can be no standing still. In his novel *To Be a Pilgrim* Joyce Cary writes that we must renew ourselves or die. We must make new worlds about us for the old does not last. 'Those who cling to this world must be dragged backwards into the womb which is also the grave. We are the pilgrims who must sleep every night beneath a new sky, for either we go forward to the new camp or the whirling earth carries us to the one behind. There is no choice but to move, forwards or backwards.'

One Makes a Path by Walking

Too often, and especially when we are younger, we imagine we are called to play the lead in our own dramas. Only slowly do we learn that there are also small-part players, under-studies who never get a chance to go on but must always hold themselves in readiness, and also those other crucial figures backstage: the stage managers, stagehands, fly-men and electricians: each has a role to play, however small.

There is a story that illustrates this. It is about a celebrated production of Shakespeare's *King Lear*, starring John Gielgud, and directed by Harley Granville-Barker. In the production was an actor who played the part of a Captain, a practically non-existent role which called for him to follow Lear on at the end of the play. He has one line to speak, after Lear's wonderful lines: 'Now she's gone forever! Cordelia! Cordelia! Stay a little. Ha! What is't thou says't? Her voice was ever soft, gentle and low, an excellent thing in a woman. I killed the slave that was a-hanging thee.' To which the Captain replies, ''Tis true, my lord, he did.' In the rehearsal the actor said his line, neither ill nor well, he just said it. Granville-Barker then called him to one side and said quietly, 'That is an extremely important line. You must let the audience *feel* you have seen a miracle – you *have* – you are not accustomed to miracles – you are a rough soldier. The only other line you have is,

'If it be a man's work, I'll do it.' That has established your character and now you have seen with your own eyes a very old man, at the point of death, kill a man with his own hands, pick up the body of his daughter – and a dead body is very difficult to carry. You have seen a thing that is not possible, yet you have seen it – your heart must beat faster when you say, "'Tis true, my lord, he did." It must be with an awareness that almost stops Lear's rage for a second – he must *feel* you there and turn to *you* as he says, "Did I not, fellow?" Now go away and think about it.'

In life, as in the theatre, every word we speak, every gesture, every action, every step we take, is of significance. And on the spiritual journey we have to keep walking, setting one foot in front of the other. As Thomas Merton wrote, 'If you forget everything else that has been said, I would suggest you remember this for the future: From now on everybody stands on his own feet.'

There is an exercise I sometimes use in my workshops and retreats which involves walking as a form of meditation. It requires a large space, a studio or a hall, as it involves unrolling scrolls of white lining paper to a length of 30 or 40ft, fixed at either end with weights. In front of each scroll is a bowl of paint into which each person dips their feet. They then have to walk the length of the scroll, slowly and with great concentration. I say this because it would be very easy to approach the exercise cynically, or superficially, walking swiftly from end to end, saying, 'So what?' But if it is done in the right attitude of openness and concentration it becomes a Zen-like ritual of great beauty because the scroll represents each person's life. At the start the individual looks ahead at the expanse of white paper, conscious of the distance that has to be travelled, with a heightened awareness of each footmark about to be made, whether with the whole foot, half foot, heel or toes. Often those doing the exercise, having reached half-way, pause to look back, perhaps conscious that half their life is over and that now, as they walk the last stretch, they are approaching their old age. When the exercise is completed everyone returns to the starting point to meditate on their scroll of life. Such is the impact of this simple ritual-meditation that always everyone asks to take their own scroll away with them.

This exercise serves as a reminder that we come this way but once. The calligraphy created by the feet is often also very revealing. My most vivid memory is of a woman who, after only a few years of a very happy marriage lost her husband to cancer. When she had completed her scroll of life we were all suddenly aware of how, throughout the exercise she had kept to one side of the paper, unconsciously leaving a space for another set of footprints, those of her husband. It was indeed a very powerful expression of her bereavement and loneliness without the one with whom she had been accustomed to walk.

Towards the end of Paul Auster's novel *Moon Palace* the protagonist sets off to walk, without interruption, towards the Pacific, borne along by a growing sense of happiness. 'Once I reached the end of the continent I felt that some important question would be resolved for me. I had no idea what that question was, but the answer had already been formed in my steps, and I had only to keep walking to know that I had left myself behind, that I was no longer the person I had been.'

One makes a path by walking!

One Equal Music

Mozart's *Piano Concerto for Two Pianos*, K.365 was being performed in the Cadogan Hall in London by some eighty young musicians each of whom was from a different geographical and cultural background; each with their own ambitions, problems, and differences; yet they were as one with the music, achieving a unity in diversity, transcending their individual selves, so that Mozart's music could flow through them. Watching and listening to them I thought of a passage from Vikram Seth's novel, *An Equal Music*, in which the members of a quartet are playing the first contrapuntus of Bach's *Art of Fugue*:

> We play with such intensity, such calm, as I never imagined we could either feel or create. The fugue flows on and our travelling bows follow its course, guided and guiding. Our synchronous visions merge and we are one; with each other, with the world, and with that long dispersed being whose force we receive through the shape of his notated vision and the single swift flowing syllables of his name.

Later, reflecting on this experience, it seemed to me a perfect metaphor for what happens in the practice of meditation when a group of people come together for that purpose. All differences of personality or outlook are merged in the concentrated silence. The concerns of the ego fall away and in the process a very powerful silence ensues. Those meditating have heard the silence beyond the silence. Then at the end of the meditation each person emerges slowly, like a swimmer rising to the surface, or a mountaineer having reached the summit. At first no one wants to speak, so powerful is this sense of a shared harmony in which they have been the instruments played upon – like an Aolian harp hanging from a tree, played by the breezes.

Seated in the Cadogan Hall, my mind went back to hearing Rosalyn Tureck play Bach's *Goldberg Variations* transcribed for the piano. The entire work, with repeats, lasts almost an hour and a half. At the end, as the audience erupted into cheers, Tureck continued to sit at the piano, unmoving, before finally turning to acknowledge the applause. It was as though she and the music had become one. Indeed she once said that as she lowered her hands to play the opening notes of the *Goldberg Variations* she already heard in her head the closing notes. Such a performance was in itself a profound meditation. It is the same when an artist such as Nigel Kennedy plays the *Elgar Violin Concerto:* he and the violin and Elgar's music become one.

 35

Meditation and the Market Place

Looking along the bookshelves marked 'Holistic', or visiting a Mind, Body, Spirit Fair, or even watching such television programmes as *Spirituality Shopper*, one is bombarded with claims for meditation as a 'feel good' therapy that will even improve one's sex life, or make one more successful at work. At a popular level meditation is ubiquitous. It is rather like the mantra used by Capital FM Radio promising 'twenty-four hours of relaxing music'. Of course music can be relaxing and set one's feet dancing but, as Daniel Barenboim pointed out in his Reith Lectures, the true appreciation of music requires, as does meditation, a total response. And so the true practice of meditation calls for the essential element of discipline: persevering whether we feel like it or not and a commitment to a journey – the end result of which should be the inner transformation of our being and not simply self-improvement. But there are hazards on the way. One can meet individuals who have meditated for years, in ashrams in India, in monasteries and convents, and yet all it has done for them is to inflate their egos, while some become so detached that they are as complacent as the Cheshire Cat, untouched by the pain or distress of others.

All spiritual teachers, all mystics, have warned of such hazards but how are we to avoid them? Ideally it is by having a teacher but true teachers are not that plentiful. We can, of course, go on a retreat, to sit at the feet of a true master such as Thich Nhat Hanh, or spend a week at those monasteries, such as Worth Abbey, which run special courses. Above all we need to exercise a watchfulness – for ultimately it is a matter of humility and, as T.S. Eliot reminds us, 'Humility is endless'!

One of the fruits of meditation is silence: not a dead silence but a living silence that acts like a powerful energy. And it is in those situations in life when words prove inadequate that the silence born out of meditation can prove most healing. One of the areas in which the practice of meditation is proving of benefit is in the field of psychotherapy. Peter Conradi, the author of *Going Buddhist*, comments in a paper entitled 'Calm – Abiding Meditation and Ox-herding Pictures': 'Where I have witnessed the benign effects of meditation is in psychotherapy, to which it is kin. There are therapists who, knowledgeable about meditation, invite their clients to practise it and also therapists who report finding it clinically useful themselves: the therapist is able to go deeper, to relax in difficult sessions, to handle the counter-transference with skill.'

One such therapist is Dr Monica Lanyado who, in a paper for the American Journal: *Psycho-analytic Perspectives*, December 2008, entitled 'Dwelling in the present moment: an exploration of the resonances between transitional experiences and meditational states', describes the case of Gail who, while eighteen at the time of her writing, had been coming to her for six years. Abandoned by her mother when she was four, her subsequent disruptive emotional development and behavioural and emotional difficulties meant that being with her was 'like sitting on the edge of a rumbling volcano. She was highly re-active and likely to blow into a tantrum or temper over tiny mis-attunements on my part to her state of mind. Most of the time I was on 'red alert' during her sessions and felt tense in anticipation of them and worn out at the end of them.' Over time, however, Dr Lanyado, who has practised meditation for many years, found that increasingly she was able simply to 'be' with Gail, without talking, for longer periods with her, 'in the way that during meditation practice one of the simplest aims is to sit still and try to quiet the mind and 'be' rather than 'do'.' With practice she found it possible to keep this centre of calm for increasing periods of time in her sessions with Gail and similarly Gail began to respond to this. One of the outcomes of meditation, she concludes, is that out of stillness and quietness an essential simplicity can emerge which feeds into everyday living and being.

I was reminded of all this when, a few years ago, I visited a primary school outside London in a particularly deprived area. On arrival we were invited to join one class for its Candle Time which was about to begin. There were about twenty children, aged nine, of varying ethnic backgrounds. Music was playing – some Arvo Part – as we entered. The teacher was seated in a corner while the children were in pairs: one seated while the second child stood behind, gently massaging their partner's head, neck and shoulders. They then changed places. When this simple ritual was completed the teacher invited the children to sit on the floor and to close their eyes while she read them the passage from the Gospels, 'Except a grain of wheat fall into the ground and die, it cannot live.' She proceeded to lead them in a guided meditation, inviting them to imagine themselves as grains of wheat being carried in a large sack when, suddenly, the sack is emptied and each of them falls into a dark place. At this point she asked them to open their eyes and to share any experience they might have had of being in such a dark place. One small boy said that it was when he saw his father beat up his mother. A girl said that it was when she said goodbye to her grandmother in Zimbabwe, knowing she would never see her again. Another boy said it was when he saw his father weep for the first time. The teacher then led the children back into the meditation, asking them to imagine the grain of seed in the ground beginning to send down roots and to push up a green blade towards the surface, towards light, towards hope. How many of them had had that experience?

The emotional literacy of those children, most of whom were from very disturbed families and backgrounds was remarkable. They were encouraged to share feelings which children in general and boys especially, rarely admit to. In adult life how many problems in relationships are due to people being unable to articulate their feelings. All this owed much to that particular teacher who had trained as a counsellor and who practised meditation, but also to the youthful headmistress. From her I learned that from the very moment the children entered the school they were made to feel that it was their school and so, when the Mayor, the Bishop, or any VIP, came to visit, it would be the children and not the staff who would show the visitor around. Even when we arrived I noticed how warmly the children waved and smiled at us, and whenever we entered a classroom would invite us to take a seat. The children were also taught that it is OK to be angry but not to be destructive. In one of the classrooms where their paintings hung on a line like washing I noticed one entitled

'The angry Jesus'. The head teacher told me of one new boy who was so disturbed when he arrived that he automatically expected to be told off. As a result his defences were always up and he was constantly looking for a fight. One day she said to him, 'I see you are very cross. Do you want to come and sit down in my study and be calm?' Then she left him alone. When she returned he said, 'A funny sort of school this!' at which point she knew that she had won him over simply by giving him space to be angry. Now he was one of the school monitors.

Looking at the children's art work which was on display I could see how open, imaginative and insightful they were becoming. One of them had written: 'One of the things I have learned is that every person, whatever their age and position in the school family has an important and vital role to play. I am going to read a poem that speaks about that. Sam.' As the headmistress emphasised, the key words were: openness and security. 'The children know that whatever is said is held in confidence.'

In that school clearly each of the teachers knew how to be still and listen. As Dr Monica Lanyado remarks, 'One of the outcomes of meditation is that out of stillness and quietness a clarity and a simplicity can emerge which feeds into everyday living and being.'

36

Riding Out the Storm

A friend once wrote to tell me that her marriage was breaking up. 'These last few months have been quite dark and difficult

ones, and things have now come to a head. Roger has decided
he cannot go on living with me and he is leaving. He has
also found someone else. We have yet to tell the children.'
Four months later she wrote to tell me of several deaths in
the family. 'So many endings and goodbyes mixed in, however
with new green shoots. Strangely, despite the pain, I feel that
I must embrace and look at all this as fully as I dare while it
is all happening. A good friend quoted the following for me
from Rilke: "We may only use the strings of a lament to the
full if one is determined later to play upon them, with their
means, the whole jubilance that grows and gathers behind
everything burdensome, painful and endured, and without
which the voices are not complete."'

In Shakespeare's play of *Pericles*, at the height of a terrifying
storm, the 'sea-tossed Pericles', as Gower, the Narrator, describes
him, learns that his wife Thaisa has died at sea while giving
birth to their child Marina, and he cries out in his pain, 'Oh, ye
gods, why? / Why do you make us love your goodly gifts / And
snatch them straight away?' So, too, Job cries out to his God,
'Why dost Thou make me Thy butt, and why have I become
Thy target?' just as Jesus, in his final hour, cries, 'My God, my
God, why hast Thou forsaken me?' It is a cry that continues to
echo to this day, whether in Zimbabwe, in Darfur, in Iraq, in
New Orleans and Haiti, in Pakistan, in Sri Lanka, in Palestine,
and wherever there are floods, earthquakes, hurricanes, and
other disasters. Faced with death or loss of those we love, or
loss of home, life seems drained of all meaning.

The story of Pericles is that of a young man who sets out
on his life's journey to discover its unique meaning for him.
Ambition is nearly his undoing at the start, as a result of which
he goes into voluntary exile, only to be shipwrecked. He alone
survives, to be stranded on the shore of an unknown country.
Later, through his own wits, he wins the hand of Thaisa and sets
sail to return to his kingdom, when a second storm leads to the
death of his wife. He subsequently loses his child Marina, and

eventually his reason. He loses everything. The second part of the play follows his daughter Marina, (who, it transpires, is not dead), through her trials and vicissitudes until she discovers her life's vocation, that of a healer through the medium of music, what today we would call a music therapist. And so, at the play's great climax, Marina is brought to Pericles, not knowing he is her father and, through the power of music, restores him to sanity. It is at this moment that he hears, as it were, the music of the spheres. The final scene takes place in the temple of Diana, the reigning goddess of the play, where finally the two stories come together and we see how the destinies of father and daughter are interwoven in a final Paradisal reunion of father, mother and child. It is clearly an archetypal story, unlike any other of Shakespeare's plays, and it enacts the journey that each one of us makes. As the North American Indian shaman Jamie Highwater once said: We must not be afraid of what we are becoming.

We are ourselves the mystery which we are seeking to unravel. Each of us, like Pericles, like Marina, must go on that quest where we will learn to recognise our own depths and bring forth something that was never told before. It is only when, like Pericles, like Marina, like Job, like Jesus, we learn how to go down into our own darkness that then we encounter rebirth.

I think often of a poem written by Sidney Keyes who was not 21 when he died during the Second World War while in enemy hands in Tunisia. The poem is called *Cervières* and in it the poet is talking to two French children who are crying because the birds have eaten all their cherries. He urges them to look more closely at what has happened and counsels them to

> Regard your loss. Realise your loss.
> Planting this lump of pain, perhaps a flower
> Might burst from it, perhaps a cherry tree,

Perhaps a world or a new race of men.
The fruit is stolen and our dreams have failed.
Yet somewhere – O beyond what bitter ranges? –
A seed drops from the sky and like a bomb
Explodes into our orchard's progeny,
And so our care may colonise a desert.
Aimee and Victor, stop crying. Can't you understand
They cannot steal our cherries or our joy?
Let them take what they want, even our dreams.
Somewhere our loss will plant a better orchard.

It is here that the practice of meditation enables us, however sharp the pain, to look clearly and to 'be grateful for whoever comes' as Rumi puts in his poem, *The Guest House*. We die many times in any one life but, provided we do not block the life-force, each death leads to a rebirth, and this process continues to the very end of our lives. To be an elder, therefore, is to be one who is still learning, still growing, learning to weave together the extremes of joy and woe. Through the practice of meditation we are enabled to go through the fire and to emerge like gold that has been refined in the process.

 37

Space for Meditation

In meditating we become aware of an inner space that is vibrant with life. It is as though in the deepest part of us there is a whitewashed room with a window in each of the four walls, looking out on the Aegean seas. This cool space is empty yet full of light and the gentle stirring of the breezes bearing the scent of cedars and herbs. I think of a painting I have by Sheila O'Beney, on which I often meditate. It is in the style of a Paul Klee: a series of squares in delicate mauves, blues and greys. Two thirds of the way down, however, there is a white, unpainted square: an empty space. The painting is called 'Space for meditation'. It is this space that we enter each time we start our meditation.

'For each seeker the path will be different, because each of us is different,' writes the Sufi teacher Llewellyn Vaughan-Lee. 'There are as many ways to God as there are human beings, and this journey demands that we each make the ultimate journey. To follow the thread that is hidden in the heart is the most demanding task life can offer. And the teacher can only point the way: even the great teachers like Christ, Muhammed, and the Buddha, could do no more than Buddha's last words to Ananda: "Therefore, O Ananda, be a lantern unto yourself. Do not seek for refuge in anything else. Work on thy salvation diligently."'

Similarly Father Bede Griffiths used to counsel: 'I believe that each one of us has an inner light, an inner guide, which will lead us through the shadows and the illusions by which we are surrounded, and open our minds to the truth. It may come through poetry or art, or philosophy or science, or more commonly through encounter with people and events day by day. Personally I find that meditation, morning and evening every day, is the best and most direct method of getting in touch with reality. In meditation I let go of everything of the outer world of the senses, of the inner world of thoughts, and listen to the inner voice of the Word which comes in the silence.'

38

'I Will Arise Now, and Go to Innisfree'

It was in 1991 that, on a visit to Ireland to work with the novelist Molly Keane, I came across some ruined cottages and barns on a cliff in County Cork, facing the Irish Sea. Moved by an impulse, and the sheer beauty of the situation, almost a year later I succeeded in buying a ruin with a view. I then had the task of converting it into the hermitage which I had long dreamed of having. It became indeed, for a number of years, a very special place and I would try to spend as much time there as my work in the theatre permitted. It became for me my own Innisfree, and often I would murmur Yeats' poem:

> I will arise now, and go to Innisfree,
> And a small cabin build there, of clay and wattles made;
> Nine bean-rows will I have there, a hive for the honey-bee.
> And live alone in the bee-loud glade
> And I shall have some peace there, for peace comes dropping
> slow.

I have never forgotten some words Molly Keane wrote in a letter during one of my absences. 'Darling Jamie, I walked down the boreen this morning with Hero (her dog) to look at your house, and though the day was hideous and the sea quite unfriendly, the house was so benignant in its aspect summer could have been warming it.' It was there that I spent much time alone, and also did a great deal of writing in the large studio which served me as chapel, study, bedroom. Waking up in its high, white, raftered space, with its wide arched windows looking out to sea, it was like being in a peasant church on a remote Greek island, and from the start I had a sense of being in a new phase of my life.

May 8ᵗʰ 1994

This place has such a powerful presence, perched on its promontory like a small Celtic monastery. There is such an expanse of sea and sky and the very solitariness of it affects me deeply. The place challenges me, opens me outwards, feeding me at the deepest level of my being.

May 9ᵗʰ

A day of such calm, the sea moving with the slowest and gentlest of ripples, a translucent blue mirroring the almost cloudless sky. The waves softly caress the rocks below with a shushing, cradling sound. Bees and butterflies hover from plant to plant in my garden. To appreciate the gift of such a day one has to have experienced also those days of rain, enveloping mist, and wild angry winds.

May 20ᵗʰ

The great breakers heave their shoulders as though for a final assault as they race towards the rocks and then hurl themselves forward, leaping the hurdles of black rocks (where, when the tide is out, the cormorants perch), before exploding into giggles of white foam. The wind relentlessly buffets, tugging at the roof tiles. There are days when the wind blows the rain horizontally and I am always moved by the way the grasses that grow on the top of my boundary wall yield before the onslaught, yielding to the force of the wind, and then when the storm has passed stand erect again. Watching them I am reminded of the Shaker hymn: To bow and to bend we shan't be ashamed, to turn, turn, will be our delight, till by turning, turning, we come round right!'

I am like a thirsty plant soaking up the solitude here. And today my friend John Hencher writes to me:

> I often think of you in your cliff-top fastness and I visualise you most frequently sitting at the round table on the lower terrace, gazing out to sea. I hope that the remainder of your time there will be good, creative and energising. I have thought that you seemed very tired lately, so the solitude and the space for work from the inside will refresh you. More and more I value, and seek out, space and time for solitude. I find that during these times, when nothing much seems to happen, that later I have realised how much has taken place. My spiritual life is becoming increasingly still and wordless. This is not through any great effort on my part or by the use of particular techniques. It has strangely stolen upon me and I am grateful for it.

It is this last sentence which, above all, sums up one of the main fruits of the practice of meditation, and one that I learned in my hermitage. Those years there were a great privilege, but we can all find a place apart where we can be alone and know some peace. For what Yeats' poem is saying at the end is that wherever one is, 'on the roadway, or on the pavements gray', Innisfree is where one is. It is, as the American actor Ron Vawter once remarked to me about Assisi, 'Ultimately it is a place inside you. It is there, wherever you go.' It is in this solitude, like seeds underground, that new life is stirring. Only long after do we become aware of the new growth that has been quietly taking place.

39

'Look at the Stars! Look, Look up at the Skies!'

Meditation sharpens the sight and the insight and deepens our sense of wonder, whether we believe in God or not. Believers and unbelievers alike can contemplate the mystery of the universe with awe and humility. 'Look at the birds of the air!' says Jesus, and we have but to look at one bird, the jay, to perceive the mysterious workings of nature. The jay has a specialised knowledge of how best to plant oak and beech trees that still amazes the experienced forester. Left to themselves these trees cannot successfully reproduce themselves, for acorns and beechnuts would merely lie at the base where they had fallen, unable to grow well in the shade of their species. Therefore the forester has to operate artificially. The jay, however, fills its crop with acorns and beechnuts and sticks them in the soil far more skilfully than any forester. It never puts several acorns together but always at correct planting distances, often in rows. Nature repeatedly reveals to us a deeper pattern, evidence of the Eternal Mind at work. We have but to look up, to use our eyes and ears. As Francis Thompson expressed it,

> Turn but a stone and start a wing!
> 'Tis ye, 'tis your estranged faces
> That miss the many splendoured thing.

The greater reality is constantly breaking through in the most unexpected ways. In the Gospels we find it in the story of a widow's last shilling, a small boy's picnic, or friends breaking bread off the Emmaus Road. Epiphanies are everywhere: in the majesty of a night sky with its myriad of stars whether seen in the heart of Africa or on a hilltop in Wales. As a child I was taught that the night sky was a blanket and the stars holes through which we catch a glimpse of the brilliance of light on the other side. As a poetic image it evokes something of the mystery that lies beyond the immediate galaxies that we can see from our planet. Epiphanies are the breaking through of the light, not just of the Divine, but of simple insights.

It is through the cracks that light breaks through as William Blake says. Cracks disfigure the smooth surface of our lives as surely as they do a ceiling or a wall; cracks are those things that disturb us, cause us pain, anger or bewilderment. But through such painful cracks light can break through to a new epiphany. For the Christian the Eucharist itself is such a crack – the revelation of something existing in eternity. Epiphany can come upon us anywhere.

I knew it once in a tiny churchyard in Herefordshire. There had been deep snow but it had all melted by the time I drove over to celebrate the early Eucharist for the small congregation at Knill Church. Walking in the churchyard beforehand I noticed one last patch of snow in a corner. On approaching I saw that it was a clump of snowdrops that had pushed their way up through the snow. I stooped and picked a few snowdrops and took them into the church where I gave them to Becky, a small girl who had a speech impediment but who had learned to say 'Amen'. During the prayer of Consecration she began to call out 'Amen! Amen!' I stopped in the middle of the prayer and looking across to her replied, 'Amen, Becky! Amen!' and together we chanted these Amens. Everyone looked up and, instead of being irritated by her interruption, their faces broke into smiles. On that morning those few snowdrops were a moment of epiphany for Becky as they were for all of us there. The world is indeed 'charg'd with the grandeur of God,' as Manley Hopkins says. 'It will flame out like shining from shook foil.'

40

A Tree Being Motionless
Birds Come to It

There are moments on days of great calm when there is not even a breeze and not a leaf stirs that, looking up into the branches of a tree one sees, partially hidden among the leaves, a bird sitting motionless, waiting. And if, as I often do early in the morning in my garden in Wales, we sit quite still we will soon find ourselves surrounded by a carousel of winging birds, each intent on its own activities. The moment one moves, however, they all vanish and the garden is suddenly emptied of bird life.

There was a period when, as a boy, we lived in a cottage on an isolated common in Gloucestershire which was inhabited by plovers and curlews. I would spend hours lying flat, inching my way slowly towards their nests, determined to get as close as I could in order to observe them more clearly. Perhaps that is when the practice of meditation began for me? In birdwatching one has to keep very still, waiting patiently, sometimes for hours, for the bird to alight or visit its nest. Often it will not appear or we find that we have scared it away by some sudden movement. Meditation is such a waiting, a listening with half-held breath, for the coming of the Wondrous Bird. In the practice of meditation the ego learns to lie still and, in the process, our inner self becomes more deeply aware of the over-arching pattern of all life, and the sheer wonder of being.

Seated quietly in my garden I observe a spider spinning its web from one slender stalk to another, or I listen to the bumble bees at work in a clump of catmint or salvia, or observe the water-wagtail bobbing its way across the lawn like a mechanical toy. I sit and watch the house martins building a nest out of beakfuls of mud or, later on, wheeling in to feed their young just as, at dusk, while the bats emerge in pairs from under the eaves of the house. By sitting still and listening we begin to absorb the silence and to become aware, at the same time, perhaps even for the first time, of the tapestry of small sounds that lie beneath the silence. Such listening is the beginning of meditation.

In Marguerite Duras' play *The Lovers of Viorne*, the Interrogator is trying to discover what led Claire Lann to commit an appalling murder. Again and again he is thwarted by her responses. The final words of the play, spoken by Claire, are, 'If I were you, I'd listen. Listen!' Like the Interrogator most of us are often too busy analysing and asking questions so that we never hear the answers in the silences.

To enter silence is to set out upon a journey into the interior. We have only to stand in the silence of the night in open countryside, under the tapestry of stars, to realise, like Isaac Newton, 'to myself I am only a child playing on a beach while vast oceans of truth lie undiscovered before me.' It is into this silence of waiting and wonder, of just being, that certain insights will come like birds alighting for a moment on the branch of a tree. Such insights are from the heart rather than from the head. They are intuitive. As the small boy said: God is a feel, not a think! But it is not only insights that come. The more centred we are, the more rooted like a tree, we will find that certain events, certain people, will come into our orbit without our having to do anything about them.

Carl Jung loved to tell a Zen Buddhist story about people in a remote part of China who were experiencing a severe drought, so that their crops were threatened, and no amount of prayers or offerings had any effect. And so the people sent for a holy man, asking him to pray for rain. After three days the rains came. But the people were mystified because all that the holy man appeared to do was to sit in his cave. 'But what did you do?' they asked, and he replied, 'First I put myself in order and then all Nature is in order around me!'

It is as Lao Tzu says:

On the way to knowledge
Many things are accumulated.
On the way to wisdom
Many things are discarded.
Less and less effort is used
Until things arrange themselves.

The writer Pearl Binder (Lady Elwyn Jones) once remarked, 'I always travel slowly and obscurely on cargo ships and slow trains. I travel for the sake of what I see on the way.' Today, however, we are more concerned with getting as quickly from A to Z. How rarely on a train journey do we see people looking out of the window at the passing scenery? They are more likely to be on their mobiles or texting.

There are days in Wales when, seated at my window, the hills and woods are ablaze with sunlight and colour; and there are other days when the sun is clouded and all colour drained away from the landscape. And so we learn to accept the changing weather of our own moods and circumstances, allowing ourselves to be changed by events. A tree in winter is not dead but simply awaiting the return of spring when it will put forth new leaves and birds will come again to nest in its branches.

Once, in New York, a group of business executives were taking part in a workshop led by a therapist. Each was invited to imagine themselves as a tree growing from seed, and to identify with the life of that tree. At the end of the exercise they were invited to speak about the experience. One of the men described how he had not known what tree he was meant to be and so he lay curled up, imagining himself as a seed and waiting to discover what kind of tree he would grow into. He never got beyond that stage. Clearly the visualisation had resulted in his having to face up to the fact that he had not yet found his true direction in life, and that it was only by being still and waiting that he might hope eventually to find in what direction he should be going.

Society can only be renewed by renewing individuals and in order to do this we have to give individuals, starting with children in schools, an opportunity to contact their own inner resources. As Ira Progoff wrote, we gradually discover that our life has been going somewhere, however blind we have been to its direction, and however unhelpful to it we ourselves have been: 'We find that a connective thread has been forming beneath the surface of our lives, carrying the meaning that has been trying to establish itself in our existence. It is the inner continuity of our lives. As we recognise and identify with it, we see an inner myth that has been guiding our lives unknown to ourselves.'

With Progoff's reference to the thread we return to Blake's lines,

> I give you the end of a golden string;
> Only wind it into a ball,
> It will lead you in at Heaven's gate,
> Built in Jerusalem's wall.

 41

A Field of Stillness

What do we mean when we say 'The sky is blue'? The sky may be green, grey, mauve, crimson, orange, black, white, or blue, according to the time and the season of the year. So the question is: How can we see the blue of the sky before we say

'The sky is blue'? This is the theme of a poem by the American poet Wallace Stevens:

> You must become an ignorant man again
> And see the sun with an ignorant eye
> And see it clearly in the idea of it …
> The sun must bear no name – but be –
> In the difficulty of what it is to be.

And so the question also is: How can we see those about us before we affix the labels: mother, father, lover, child, teacher, leader? Sadly, all too often, after a time, so many husbands and wives, parents and children, teachers and students, no longer look at or into each other. They see the label and not the person, and then they are surprised when the relationship falls apart! How rarely do politicians and their think tanks see people as individuals and not as statistics? Labels pin people down like butterflies in a frame, except of course that people cannot be compartmentalised like this for eventually they will rebel. We fix the label and cease to look and so do not see that the person is changing, growing, or withering. In the same way, few people listen to one another because they are too busy making their own sound, waiting to interrupt with their own noise.

We need to learn how to listen stethoscopically, to catch the things that people want to say but can't, as well as to determine the value of what is actually being said. Many politicians, leaders and preachers may appear to be saying the right thing and yet intuitively we often recognise that theirs are hollow words. They are not speaking authentically, from the heart, but from the party line. We have to learn how to look long and deep and not be afraid of what we may find. It is through the practice of meditation that we begin to experience the is-ness of all things and see them in their entirety.

A great deal of the joy that children bring is their power of seeing the world as a new thing. What children do for us to renew for us the freshness of that first vision which Thomas Traherne so movingly describes: 'The corn was orient and immortal wheat, which never should be reaped, nor was ever sown I thought it had stood from everlasting to everlasting ... all things abided eternally, as they were in their proper places.' Sadly children almost always lose this power as soon as they begin their education. It is said that when you give a child the name of a bird it loses the bird. It never sees the bird again but only a sparrow, a thrush, a swan. It no longer sees the thing but only the label.

It is a common experience that when we emerge from a meditation that we often see people and things as if for the first time, each in its own essence. In his book, *The Power of Now*, Eckhart Tolle writes, 'The plant that you have in your house, have you ever truly looked at it? Have you allowed that familiar yet mysterious being called 'plant' to teach you its secrets? Have you noticed how it is surrounded by a field of stillness? The moment you become aware of a plant's emanation of stillness and peace that plant becomes your teacher.'

The practice of meditation will inevitably lead us to a deeper awareness of all things and of one another, as well as of the sub-text to every meeting as we begin to hear those words of secret Silence.

42

The Lark Ascending

A short walk from where I live on the borders of Wales and England I am high up in the hills. Ahead of me are the Black Mountains of Wales while on the English side are the Malvern Hills of Worcestershire, and further round are Housman's 'blue remembered hills' of Shropshire. Up there are buzzards circling, even occasionally a Red Kite and, if one stops to listen and then look up, there high, high up in the sky is a small black dot: it is the skylark. How vividly Vaughan Williams catches, in the closing bars of his work, *The Lark Ascending*, that quality of hovering ecstasy. Thinking about this I am reminded of a phrase used by Sigmund Freud in his recommendations to those practising psychoanalysis. Rather than taking detailed notes of each patient, he advocated 'simply not directing one's attention to anything in particular, and in maintaining *an evenly hovering attention* in the face of all that one hears.'

Similarly in meditation we do not direct our attention to anything in particular, not even the mantra, but as the author of *The Cloud of Unknowing* wrote, 'See that nothing remains in your conscious mind but a naked intent reaching out to God, not clothed in any particular thought about God but only that He is as He is. Let God be as He is. Don't dress Him up.' And so both the practising therapist or psychoanalyst and the meditator, learn to practise this 'hovering awareness', as Christopher MacKenna observed in his paper for the *British Journal of Psychotherapy*, Vol. 24, November 2008. There is, however, a difference for while the psychoanalyst must be alert to the significant detail, the unexpected silence, or something that perhaps, in a welter of personal detail, is unsaid; in meditation, it is important to gently disengage from all thought. This is why our medieval author entitled his work *The Cloud of Unknowing* for it is only when, in meditation, we are prepared to let go of all thought and simply rest in a state of being, what Eckhart Tolle refers to as 'the power of Now', in a state of hovering attention like that of the lark, that we shall then gradually begin to see our landscape in its entirety. Emptying ourselves of all thought, we hover in space. But it is often when we emerge from our meditation, like a swimmer from the sea, that new insights then appear, or a different reading of a current situation, as we see beyond the clutter of our daily human tangles.

We live in a time of such fragmentation that we are in danger of losing touch with all meaning. As G.K. Chesterton observes in his poem, *The Wise Men*:

> Oh, we have learned to peer and pore
> On tortured puzzles from our youth.
> We know all labyrinthine lore –
> We are the three wise men of yore.
> And we know all things but the truth.
> We have gone round and round the hill
> And lost the wood among the trees
> And learnt long names for every ill.

And so, as Chesterton observes later in the poem,

> Step softly under snow or rain
> *To find the place where men can pray.*
> The way is all so very plain
> That we may lose the way.

Resting in silence we wait, like a naturalist waiting for a bird to emerge from its nest and we may find that truth is revealed in unexpected ways. Many years ago, when I first began to meditate, I was in the throes of founding and running the

Hampstead Theatre in London when, on one occasion, I was faced with a crisis involving a whole production team which I handled clumsily. In order to escape the problem I went away for a few days to stay in the country. Lying on my bed that first afternoon, half asleep, I experienced a particular nightmare that I had not had since childhood which always took the form of a small boulder hurtling through space at a great speed, coming closer and closer to me until, at the moment that it was about to crush me, I would awake screaming. On this occasion, however, being half awake, I decided to wait and see what would happen. Lying there with my eyes closed, I felt the enormous weight of the giant boulder settle on my stomach. As I breathed deeply in and out in order to relieve the weight so, slowly, it grew lighter and became like a large balloon full of air, inside which I saw clearly the words: RETURN TO LONDON. I got up, packed my bag and at once drove back to London to face the music and deal with an ugly situation which was primarily my fault.

It is often in such unexpected ways that intuitions reveal themselves. Time and again it is as though there is a deeper wisdom beyond the wisdom of the world. It is as though, when out walking on the hills, listening to the skylarks rising above the new green corn shoots, rising ever higher out of sight – 'the lark at Heaven's gate sings' as Shakespeare describes it – that suddenly we see the world from a different perspective. All distractions fall away and, as in Gerard Manley Hopkins' poem, we see the 'landscape plotted and pieced'. Everything falls into place and we know what we must do. As a wise woman once said to a friend of mine, 'When you feel down, look at a bird flying above you. Take off occasionally with strong pinions. Go above things and look down with better perspective from time to time. Think pinions!'

43

And Darkness Lay Upon the Face of the Earth

The season of Advent prompts some reflections that are relevant to our practice of meditation. In a time of winter darkness Advent (from the Latin: *advenire*) is a looking forward in anticipation to the birth of the Child who is to be a Light-Bearer: 'The light shines in the darkness and the darkness cannot overwhelm it.' It is at this time of the year that we are also reminded of that sentence from The Old Testament which Handel uses in his great oratorio, *The Messiah*: The people that sat in darkness have seen a great light.

Why is it that darkness is generally associated with evil and light with good? Especially if, as it says in the Book of Genesis, it is believed that God created darkness and light, night and day. It is, surely, a residue of ancient fears. If there is a power cut and we are without matches or a torch, we quickly become disorientated. If we are in the country, out of doors, on a night without moon or stars, we soon lose all sense of direction. Unable to see our way forward we quickly succumb to atavistic fears of wild and predatory animals, conjuring up such phrases as 'Your enemy the Devil goeth about as a roaring lion, seeking whom he may devour.'

But all of this is a projection, for the real darkness – that of fear or uncertainty – is inside us. And so we come to the key word in that sentence from the Old Testament: The people that *sat* in darkness have seen a great light. They sat, they waited, they endured. And by waiting, by enduring such times of darkness, we learn that within the darkness a secret activity is at work. Nature herself teaches us this. If, in the countryside, on a night without stars or moon, we stand still and listen, we shall become aware of the soft drip of moisture from twigs, of the occasional murmur of roosting birds, or the snuffle of a badger or a hedgehog, the bark of a fox, the sudden squeak of a shrew caught by a silently swooping owl, or the tiny squeak of bats. We become aware of the secret activity of sap rising in trees, shrubs and plants. Above all, Nature teaches us that the longest night is always followed by the dawn. In life it is often when we are in the dark, whether of failure, betrayal, bereavement, redundancy, of illness or when we don't know what to do and are in despair, that the real work is being done in the depths of the unconscious. This secret activity of darkness is dramatically expressed in the Book of Genesis. It is in the sentence, 'And darkness lay upon the face of the earth'. In those words one senses a moment of held breath, a moment of waiting in anticipation which precedes all acts of creation. Then come the startling words, 'And God said, 'Let there be Light! And there was Light!'

But the Genesis myth is not only an attempt to explain the birth of Creation but also the birth of Consciousness in mankind. The Buddha commanded his followers, 'Be ye lanterns unto yourselves'. While Jesus said, 'Ye are the light of the world.' Each one of us carries a single lamp for humanity. In meditation we open ourselves to the light until it penetrates every corner of our being.

 44

The Hasidic Link

Over the past 50 years the practice of meditation in one form or another has spread all over the world. It has even been proved scientifically to improve people's health as well as to lower one's blood pressure. Much of the teaching has come primarily through the Buddhist and Hindu traditions although, as I have already indicated, it is there also in Islam. What, however, is less known is that for hundreds of years it has played a central role in the Kabbalah, the mystical tradition of Judaism, and which taught that the only way to resolve the warring opposites in us, and the ceaseless chatter of the mind, was through meditation. Believing that we are born with a Transcendent Self that can rise above material wants, and become more aware of the unused potentialities within each of us, the Kabbalah developed various methods of meditation to suit different temperaments. The common aim of each was to focus on the present moment by concentrating on whatever sound, word or image the chosen method advocated: in other words, what is called in Asia, one-pointedness.

The Book of Zohar (a word which can be translated as 'brilliance' or 'splendour') teaches that there are tens of thousands of worlds in the cosmos 'for there we find door within door, grade behind grade, through which the glory is made.' Centuries later Swedenborg would apply his scientific mind to the unconscious and in his remarkable conversations with angels celebrate these intuitive beliefs.

The Baal Shem Tov, founder of the Hasidic movement in Judaism, taught that we must learn to see beyond the trivial happenings of everyday life and look beyond us. It is here, also, that time and again, poets have invited us to see the world through other eyes, from Wordsworth's 'Our souls have sight of that immortal sea which brought us hither' to Francis Thompson's

Turn but a stone and start a wing!
'Tis ye, 'tis your estranged faces
That miss the many-splendoured thing

The central call, emphasised by all the Hasidic teachers, is to wake up from our inner sleep or torpor.

In the beginning of the nineteenth century Rabbi Nachman of Bratslav, like his contemporary William Blake who could see 'eternity in a grain of sand', had had certain mystical experiences that shaped his view of the entire cosmos. He felt the presence of the divine in every living thing. Like Blake he blamed idle intellectualism as a false road to knowledge and believed that it was by way of the heart that we could arrive at true wisdom. He would have agreed with Lao Tzu when he wrote, 'Forget knowledge, and you will remember all you need to know.' Above all, like the Buddha, he encouraged people to be happy and to cultivate a positive attitude to life. 'Always be joyful,' he said, 'no matter what you are. With happiness you can give a person life.' In this way, he taught, we will become more receptive to the mystery all around us. Moments of wonderful happiness and peace do not arrive simply by chance but relate to our characteristic make-up. We are not passive recipients of our experiences but we create them each day. However, if we allow ourselves to sink into self-pity, depression, or sadness, we shut out these experiences. In the eternal scheme of things we shall be judged by what we have made of ourselves. 'The quality of this life,' wrote Swedenborg, 'is the quality of *each* of us.' And what he has to say about the afterlife we find also in the Hasidic teachings which state that what we think or dream about in daily life will determine what our subsequent state and awareness will be. This concept, unlike that of mainstream Christianity, is central to the Kabbalah. It pervades the *Zohar. The Book of Splendour*, for instance, tells us repeatedly that, depending on our strivings in this world is our life hereafter. The Kabbalah does not posit the existence of one heaven and one hell but teaches, as does Swedenborg, that after death there are an infinite number of realms of consciousness. As the *Zohar* says, 'For there are many abodes prepared by the Holy One, blessed be He, each one according to his grade.'

Once, out of a meditation, there came to me the following words, which I had calligraphed for me by the artist John Rowlands Pritchard, and which hang by the side of my bed in Wales: God is an endless journey.

 45

From the Realms of Glory

The practice of meditation will deepen our awareness of the many-splendoured reality which is all about us. We will become increasingly aware that we are not alone, that there are angels and spirits all about us. A hundred years ago few people would have believed that we would fly about the world in aeroplanes and spaceships, while less than fifty years ago who would have believed that men would walk on the moon? Such feats seemed no more than the imaginings of a Jules Verne or an H.G. Wells. Yet the incredible has become credible within the space of one lifetime.

How strange then that our generation should find it difficult to believe in angels! For thousands of years people believed in the existence of winged messengers who commuted between eternity and time. For centuries the Christian Church, as did other religious cultures, believed in them. Their appearances are recorded in history and scripture, while their forms have been carved and painted in countless cathedrals, churches and temples throughout the world. And still today, even to people who are non-believers, angels continue to manifest themselves in dreams as they did centuries ago. Yet rarely today within the Churches do we hear much about angels. Are they now taboo? Did they suddenly go out with technology? Certainly it would seem as though they are suddenly not very fashionable. It apparently does not worry the angels for they continue to manifest themselves. For myself I do not say I believe in angels any more than I say that I believe in electricity, in atoms, or in the stars in the night sky. I cannot tell how these things work. I cannot even see them at work – but I know that they are there. I recall asking a very conservative Harley Street specialist what he thought about acupuncture. To my surprise he answered, 'Oh, there's no doubt it works. We just don't know how, that is all!' So, too with angels. They are there but we cannot explain them.

It is possible that angels, (the word means 'messengers') come from the unconscious, that repository of wisdom that lies beyond the intellect; but I do not discount, any more than does the biologist Rupert Sheldrake, that there may be angelic powers in outer space, that each star has its intelligence, for angels belong to another order of time and space. My own experience, however, teaches me, reassures me, that the universe is full of presences, of winged messengers – whatever we choose to call them. The word 'angel' like the word 'God' is only an image pointing to the reality behind; we could as easily use another word or, like C.S. Lewis, invent a new name for them – 'eldrils' – as he does in *Voyage to Venus*. These intelligences intervene and act on our behalf. Children are often closer to this world, as are the elderly, the very sick, and those in moments of extreme danger, exaltedness, fatigue, or the deep quiet of meditation. At such moments we hear and sense a presence. We know that we are not alone. The veil that divides this world from the next is at times almost transparent. At such times we have a glimpse of the now-ness of eternity, which is beyond time and space.

If throughout history people have described angels as clothed in white, with wings, and radiant, these are but attempts by the imagination to convey something of the speed, the intensity and the luminosity with which such messages, insights and intuitions are conveyed to us. And if all this seems strange to us we have but to recall the words of St Paul, 'The hidden wisdom of our God that we teach in our Mysteries, the things that no eye has seen, no ear has heard, things beyond the mind of man, that the spirit hath revealed.' It is in the same spirit that Hamlet rebukes his fellow student of Wittenberg University when he says, 'There are more things in heaven and earth, Horatio, than are dreamt of in your philosophy!'

Angels, archangels, cherubim and seraphim – the ancient teachings suggest that there are many ranks and many tasks for the angelic host – are not out there but, as Francis Thompson reminds us,

> Not where the wheeling systems darken,
> And our benumbed conceiving soars!
> The drift of pinions, would we hearken,
> Beats at our clay-shuttered doors!

And to some is appointed the task of looking after us: to each of us an unseen companion, assisting us on our journey through time to eternity. 'Behold, I send an angel before you, to guard you on your way, and to bring you to the place which I have prepared. Give heed to him and hearken to his voice.'

 46

'The Roses Became My Meditation'

High on a hill a few miles outside Worcester, with the Welsh and Malvern hills in the distance, stands a square red-brick building, like a miniature barracks, with a belfry and a clock tower. The monastery of St Mary at the Cross, Glasshampton, is the former stables of a great house that no longer exists. It is now the contemplative house for the Anglican Franciscans, and is reached by a winding farm track through fields. It was there that I was sent by the Bishop of Hereford, John Easthaugh, in the late 1970s, to be prepared for ordination.

February 4ᵗʰ 1978

Seated before supper in the darkened chapel at Glasshampton Monastery, near Worcester, I reflect on darkness. It seems to me that when we speak of evil we should avoid the words 'dark' or 'black', for there is a beauty in darkness which is both primal and paradisal, when we sense nature at work in the universe and in its mysterious nocturnal activity. The contrast of dark and light as that of evil and good is an anthropomorphic projection. Dark and light are an inseparable part of nature.

After supper I spend another hour in the chapel. Suddenly the clock strikes nine o'clock. How time flies when one's concentration is withdrawn to a still centre and lightly held. It is like birdwatching, only that in meditation one is waiting upon that Presence which is always present even in the winter darkness.

Here at Glasshampton the seasons come and go. I have known it for nearly two years: in full summer, in snow, during the time of my Mother's death, in spring, summer, autumn, and winter. I have experienced peace here and crisis as well as growth. 'Fundamentally,' writes Thomas Merton, 'as Max Picard points out, it probably comes to this: living in silence which so reconciles contradictions within us, they cease to be a problem.'

Sunday in June 1979

A clear dawn of washed colours, a new moon, robins and blackbirds singing. During Mass a brilliant sunrise sent shafts of light through the windows of the chapel, filtering through clouds of incense. Brother David remains on afterwards, seated in the choir stalls, a brown wool plaid blanket wrapped around his shoulders – 'It belonged to a Scottish shepherd and it is more than a hundred years old. I have had it for fifty years.' He has just spent three and a half days in solitude at Freeland, the convent outside Oxford for Anglican Franciscan nuns. The Sisters had put roses in his room, along with bread, cheese, apples and coffee. 'I had no books but the roses became my meditation. They taught me how to grow old, how to let go, how to die. And some buds never developed – like some members of our Community!'

Brother David was the oldest living member of the Society of St Francis and was the Society's first Provincial Minister. Born in North Wales he had been a priest for fifty-six years and although when I knew him he was already eighty, he was extraordinarily youthful, with little grey in his hair which kept falling across his forehead in a boyish lock. Tiny and wren-like in his movements, he took his turn in the laundry and washing up after meals. He and I would sometimes spend as long as five or six hours in the chapel. I had asked to come to a place where I might have a Zen-like preparation for the priesthood, a place of quiet, prayer, study and manual work. I absorbed so much just by being at Glasshampton, but most of all I learned from the long hours of shared silence in the chapel with Brother David. It is less what a person says and rather what a person is. One learns so much just by being still.

47

'Death Was Like a Game
I Could Not Win'

It sometimes takes a sudden illness, loss of job, bereavement, to jerk us into an awareness of the present moment and to question where we are heading. For the renowned rugby player Jonny Wilkinson it was a series of injuries that he suffered between 2003 and 2007 which prevented him from playing a single game for England. Until then his approach to playing had been so obsessive that, as he admits, 'I did not know what it meant to be really happy.' During this time, in an attempt to keep his despair at bay, he learned to play various instruments as well as to speak French and Spanish until, via quantum physics, he came to Buddhism and the practice of meditation. Until then he had been driven by a fear of failure and did not know how to free himself from it. 'Failure is one thing,' he now says, 'but Buddhism tells me that it is up to us how we interpret that failure. The Middle-Way of Buddhism is about seeing everything as inter-connected: success, failure; victory, defeat.'

When asked if he had managed to uncover the reason for his fear of failure he replied, 'I think it was rooted in an even deeper fear of death. I couldn't figure out how to avoid death. It was like a game I could not win. But my faith has given me a handle on it, based around the ideas of birth and karma. It has also given me the ability to understand that rugby, like life, will also come to an end. I guess I had been trying to block that out, hoping that it would last for ever. But I have accepted that my career will end one day and I am now in a place that will enable me to make that transition comfortably.

My fulfilment is no longer about self-gratification, it is about seeing the happiness of others.'

On bad days we learn to say, 'Today I feel lousy – it will pass!' On good days we learn to say, 'Today I feel wonderful – it will pass!' Everything is in a state of change, such is the law of the Tao, a constant waxing and waning. As one door closes another opens. Breathing in, breathing out, we learn to let go, to go with the drift of things, to accept the unfolding of our own destiny. Learning to let go of all expectations is perhaps the greatest wisdom. We breathe in and we breathe out until, one day, we breathe out for the last time and, at that moment, our spirit is released from our body.

The practice of meditation teaches us how to observe and ponder what is unfolding in the psyche and not to interfere in the process. If I cut my hand, thousands of cells are set to work to heal it. If I keep removing the bandage to see how it is faring this will hinder the process. Similarly with the psyche: we must allow it to go about its own work. If we have a problem we put it to one side while we meditate and the result will be, if we are patient, that the problem in due course will resolve itself.

Dr Franz Elkisch, my former Jungian analyst, to whom I owe so much, referring to the magnificent oaks and beeches nearby, once commented, 'If the tree had an ego and could speak, I would ask it "Where did you get your great beauty? How did you grow so tall?" and the tree would reply, "By doing nothing." One must allow things to happen.'

That, of course, is the hardest thing for all of us! Yet Lao Tzu reminds us how, in the pursuit of wisdom, less and less effort is used 'until things arrange themselves.'

48

Crossings and Crossroads

Rituals if performed with passion and devotion will always enhance our capacity to live life to the full which is why we find rituals not only in every religion, but in every aspect of life, marking as they often do key milestones in our journey, from birth to death. New rituals will always evolve but the ancient rituals and liturgies are also capable of rediscovery. Among many Christians the sign of the Cross has become a perfunctory gesture, even verging on mindless superstition. And yet if we open ourselves to its deeper meaning it can, once again, come alive and be seen not only as the central symbol of Christianity but a profound archetype for everyone, for this crossroads sign, this meeting-of-the-opposites, is to be found in many cultures and throughout history. For those who feel drawn to rediscover the sign of the Cross as a meaningful ritual, it is necessary first of all to centre down in meditation, allowing the breath to come in like the advancing tide and then to withdraw. Then, when we feel truly centred, we can begin our exploration.

Traditionally the right hand goes to the forehead on the words 'In the name of the Father'. In the centre of the forehead is the chakra known as 'the third eye'. It is through this chakra that spiritual enlightenment enters. It is interesting that in the famous portrait of St Dominic, the founder of the Catholic Church's intellectual Order, he is portrayed with a star shining just before his forehead. If now we reach up higher with the right hand, above the head, we have a sense of the Father as Abba, the Source and Origin of all things, descending from on high and entering into us. With this gesture it is as though we are drawing down power from on high: God coming down to earth and becoming human.

And now, on the words 'and of the Son', the hand descends to the level of the heart chakra which for Hindus is the centre of *bhakti* (devotion). 'The real place of the Divine Encounter,' writes Abhishiktananda, 'is in the very centre of our being, the place of our origin, from which all that we are is constantly welling up. Thus to direct the attention towards the heart, even in a physical way, is symbolically to turn all our activities towards the very centre of ourselves.' India, he remarks, has from the beginning been alive to the mystery of the heart, the *guha*, the 'cave' within, as it is called in her scriptures, the abode of Brahman, the very place of Atman itself, the source of everything. And so the hand rests at the heart, knowing that the word is made flesh in each of us, for 'the kingdom of Heaven is within'. The inner world, as Carl Jung taught, is just as real as the outside world; in fact it is more real for it is infinite and everlasting and does not change or decay as the outside world constantly does.

When we are ready, and all this should take its own time, the right hand and the left hand should move outwards to each side of the body on the words 'and of the Holy Spirit', so that the arms are outspread like the wings of a bird, an image of the Spirit brooding upon the waters of the deep before the creation of the world. Thus extended, the arms are like a gesture of compassion, embracing the entire world. Then slowly they begin to close in to encircle one's own self, nurturing the Christ within. The swing is always between reaching out to embrace the whole world and drawing in for renewal. Reaching out and drawing in, breathing in and breathing out.

There is something else to be discovered about the sign of the Cross. To cross is to signify. Those who cannot write their own names are asked to sign with a cross. It is the primordial signature as Bani Shorter observed in her paper, 'If Ritual Dies': 'Crossings and crossroads are of deep symbolic meaning in life. It was Hermes, the Messenger of the Gods, who was guardian of the crossroads in ancient Greece. There, where one is challenged by change of direction and choice, one encounters one's god, and signifies to one's self but also in relation to the Other.'

As we reach up and draw down into ourselves the strength and the power of the divine, so this movement descends in a vertical line, plunging in to the centre of our being and dissecting the horizontal line of the final gesture. The vertical line of the Other, of the Divine, of Infinity, cuts through the horizontal line of mankind and time, creating a tension of opposites. And it is at the centre of this tension that each of us has to learn to live, uniting in each of us all the opposites. The one hope for our torn world, writes Barbara Hannah in *Encounters with the Soul*, is that the warring opposites should meet. It is only when opposites are united that true peace is to be found. 'Collectively we cannot do anything for, as Jung constantly said, the only place we can do anything is in the individual, in ourselves. If we are in Tao – that place where all opposites are united – we have an inexplicable effect upon our surroundings.' If enough individuals do this and learn how to go to this inner place, they will then be able to stand the tension of the opposites outside of them.

And there are some people who stand at the crossroads of society, at a frontier, at a place not easily identifiable. The shaman, the priest, the healer, are such people. Their task is to stand at the intersection of paths and hold the tension of opposites within themselves. There at the crossroads, facing north, south, east and west, they know that the journey is in fact inwards.

❦ 49 ❦

Opening Doors and Windows of Opportunity

The tragedy of so many people's lives is that suddenly, and often too late, they are aware of having wasted their lives, of never having fulfilled their potential. A woman once wrote to me, having heard me speak on television. She was sixty-two and referred to the fact that she had only six months left to live. 'I need spiritual and mental help' she wrote. 'Till I heard you I was resigned to sitting out to the end.' Her early letters were full of anger: towards God, the Church, the World. In the course of our correspondence she revealed that at the age of eighteen she had studied art but had then developed a mental block against it, being afraid to allow herself to be spontaneous because, as she expressed it, 'spontaneity is lovely but there is a risk.' And so, rather than take that risk, she repressed her rich creativity, denied her true self, and flung herself into secretarial work, changed jobs frequently and ended up with only a state pension. 'I am left with an ability to *feel* beauty in all its forms,' she wrote, ' but no ability now to pick up pencil or brush. Too diminished and mentally exhausted to *do*, I am left with a sense of having wasted my life.'

I wrote back, suggesting she go out and buy a child's box of paints and sit down each day and paint, exactly like a child, whatever she was *feeling*, without any interference from her critical self. About two weeks later there arrived a simple, almost primitive, painting of a bowl of flowers exploding with colour. The shape was repeated underneath by a double shadow of the bowl but shaped like two large church bells with clappers. The dynamic colour of the flowers and the joyous swing of the bells expressed a powerful sense of energy and release. With the picture came a letter. 'You have reached me, reached me, *the real me*; the soft, vulnerable me, the one that wants to climb out and flow, and be a kind and loveable person, instead of tautened up, spitting aggression. I was so HAPPY!'

The relationship of creativity to spirituality is something that is still, surprisingly, little understood and often dismissed as art therapy. By spirituality I mean the development of a person's innermost self, 'the real vulnerable me.' So many, born millionaires, die in poverty. It is only by 'encouraging creative expression in everyone,' as Rowan Williams has said, 'that we help them to become fully human.' Art once belonged to ordinary communities. Such arts, as Sir Maurice Bowra, writing about primitive art, said, 'are indispensable to those who practise them. Because they give order and harmony to their sudden, over-mastering emotions and their tumbling, jostling thoughts, because they are so inextricably a part of their lives, it gives them a solid centre in what otherwise would be almost chaos.' Similarly Henry Moore wrote of such art, 'It is something made by people with a direct and immediate response to life. Sculpture and painting for them was not an activity of calculation or academism, but a channel for expressing powerful beliefs, hopes and fears.'

This is why it is important to re-awaken in people a realisation of their own creativity. We all know how much more meaningful it is to be given something that another person has made, rather than bought from an expensive boutique: a loaf of bread, a cake, a bird-table, a knitted scarf, a plant grown from seed, a surprise picnic, an embrace.

For those of us who are practising artists our task is also to open doors and windows of opportunity for others so that their lives may be enriched. Whatever gifts we have must be passed on to others, for a thing made with love is a gift of ourselves to another. Jeanette Winterson, in a radio interview with Bel Mooney, echoes what I strongly believe:

My work in this world is to open people up to the joy and the strength that is in life and in themselves. And to get people out of this littleness, this feeling of being boxed in, this feeling of being out of control. One of the reasons I am passionate about art is because it is so large and because it opens cathedrals in the mind where you can go and be and you can pray and you are not small. We have to be able to put meaning back into the lives of ordinary people.

We have to be able to put meaning back into the lives of ordinary people and to realise that every aspect of one's life, as Zen teaches, from washing dishes, preparing a meal, digging in the allotment, collecting a child from school, or helping a neighbour, is both a meditation in itself as well as an opportunity for being creative, for making something with love. Life itself is the greatest of all arts.

 50

Jimmy's Soul

Religious ideas are always and everywhere symbolic truths. They can never be understood in a rational way alone. Every religious symbol when it originated was an *experience* surpassing conscious knowledge.

It is only when religion becomes established that symbols are then worked into dogmas by the conscious intellect. An objective rational interpretation of a religious experience is of little value unless there is also a subjective and intuitive identification with the material under examination. Thus the paintings of Dame Hildergarde of Bingen, the twelfth-century mystic, erupted first from her unconscious, and only afterwards did she meditate upon them and write down the results of her meditations. The problem is that our society has largely lost touch with the art of thinking in images. 'Our thinking is largely discursive, verbal, linear', observed Joseph Campbell in his television series, *The Power of Myth*, 'yet there is more reality in an image than in a word.' Similarly Jung remarked of symbols, 'Their pregnant language cries out to us that they mean more than they say.'

At its most intense, ritual leads us into another dimension, that of the sacred. There is a remarkable example of this in Oliver Sacks' book *The Man Who Mistook His Wife For A Hat*, in which he describes Jimmy G., one of the patients at the neurological hospital in New York where Sacks was working. Admitted in 1975 at the age of 49 it was found that Jimmy could remember everything up to 1945 but everything after that date had been wiped from his memory. Such memory loss is known as Korsakov's Syndrome. Sacks wrote to Professor A.R. Luria, one of the leading Russian neurologists, asking his opinion. Luria replied:

> There are no prescriptions in a case like this. Do whatever your ingenuity and your heart suggest. There is little hope or no recovery in his memory. But a man does not consist of memory alone. He has feeling, will, sensibilities, moral being, matters of which neuro-psychology cannot speak. And it is here, beyond the realm of an impersonal psychology, that you may find ways to touch him, and change him. And the circumstances of your work allow this, for you work in a Home, which is like a little world, quite different from the clinics and institutions where I work. Neuro-psychologically there is little or nothing that you can do; but in the realm of the individual there may be much that you can do.

Sacks, finding that he tended to speak of Jimmy as 'a lost soul' wondered whether, in fact, Jimmy had been 'de-souled' by the disease. 'Do you think he has a soul?' he asked one of the nuns at the hospital. 'Watch Jimmy in chapel and judge for yourself' was the reply. He did so and was deeply moved to observe in Jimmy an intensity and a steadiness of attention and concentration that he had never witnessed before or even conceived him capable of having. He watched him kneel and take the Sacrament upon his tongue with absolute concentration and attention. He was wholly held, absorbed, by a feeling. He was totally absorbed in an act of his whole being which carried feeling and meaning in an organic continuity and unity so seamless it could not permit any break. 'Clearly,' Sacks concluded, 'Jimmy had found himself in the absoluteness of spiritual attention and act. The Sisters were right – he did find his soul there. And so was Luria whose words came back to me, 'A man does not consist of memory alone. He has feeling, will, sensibilities, a moral being ... it is here that you may touch him and see a profound change.'

Once again we return to Hamlet's words, 'There are more things in heaven and earth, Horatio, than are dreamed of in your philosophy.'

51

In the Cloud of Unknowing

One December morning in Wales I took a long walk. In the thick mist the nests of rooks appeared like dark smudges in the ghosts of trees; every bush, thorn, twig and branch had its replica in ice while the topmost twigs of a line of hawthorns glittered and sparkled in the sun like fine spun glass, and from the pine trees thick scales of ice tinkled like Japanese chimes. As I climbed the old track with the long, shaggy grass stiffly frozen, so the mist grew thicker. Telegraph wires, thickened with frost, spun the lane below like a spider's web. In the thickest part of the mist, down in the valley, although I could see nothing, I could hear the sounds of a farm beginning its day: the sudden chuckling of ducks being released, a cockerel crowing, children's voices, and cattle lowing in a barn waiting to be milked. Next came the clip-clop of a horse travelling along a lane, then over grass, then over cobbles, and a boy's voice shouting, 'Hey up!' Climbing higher still, the wind was blowing the mist along until, suddenly, a huge wall of cloud rose up, surrounding me, so that I lost all sense of direction and could go no further. I stood still, wrapped in a white blanket of mist, listening to sheep munching nearby.

It is often when all sense of direction is lost, and there are no immediate answers, that all one can do is to wait until the mists rise. It is by waiting in the cloud of unknowing, enveloped and surrounded by mystery, that the truth is often to be found, rather than in argumentative debate.

I Have a Journey Yet To Go

The practice of meditation is a journey and when we set out on it we do not know where it will lead us. We simply walk on in faith. And in meditation it is the journey and not the arriving that is important. Cafavy, the Greek poet, writes about this in his poem, *Ithaca*: 'When you set out on your journey to Ithaca,' he says, 'then pray that the road is long, full of adventure, full of knowledge.' Always, however, he insists that we must keep Ithaca in mind because to arrive there is our ultimate goal; but that when finally we do arrive there, we should not expect that Ithaca will give us riches:

> Ithaca has given you the beautiful voyage.
> Without her you would never have taken the road.
> But she has nothing more to give you.

And he concludes with these words,

> And if you find her poor, Ithaca has not defrauded you.
> With the great wisdom you have gained, with so much
>   experience,
> You must surely have understood by then what Ithacas means.

Ithaca is both a real island and a myth. As Joseph Campbell observed, we all need a myth by which to live, one that gives meaning to our lives for, as Jung also taught, each one of us has a personal myth. But as we realise and live out the blueprint of the person we are meant to be, we will become increasingly conscious that the ego has little place here, for each of us is like an instrument being played upon by some other force. It is as though the more complete and rounded an individual becomes we can hear through them that music from Beyond. As Rumi writes, 'We have fallen into the place where everything is music.'

Unthreading clover roots on my lawn, raking them over in order to expose them to the blades of the lawnmower, digging up the couch grass and ground elder, delving deep with bare hands as in a bran tub, tugging out all the white, string-like roots, attempting to unravel them, I realise it cannot all be done in a day. Once, like my father, I would have charged at the task, trying to tame the wilderness by assault, going on working for long hours hoping to see order arrive out of chaos by nightfall. Now I am more patient. I try not to seek or see the end result: just so much each day. Creating some order. I allow certain areas of wilderness, of weeds and nettles, because I will never be able to tackle it all. Yet that very disorder, that patch of untidy garden, creates its own beauty and becomes a breeding ground for moths and butterflies. I work slowly, creating a little order as I go, just keeping the wilderness at bay. I have a plan for, a vision of, my garden, how I should like it to be but, in that marvellous phrase of Mother Teresa of Calcutta, 'I do what I can.' This garden is like my life. Is each person's garden so? In which case mine will never be finished. I shall die with the weeds still rampant but where the weeds and nettles grow there will be butterflies – Peacocks, Small Tortoiseshells, Red Admirals and Painted Ladies.

I am at the age when increasingly it is natural and right to meditate on the approaching end of this stage of the journey, just as a gardener pauses at the end of a day to contemplate what has been achieved and what yet remains to be done. There is a painting by Margaret Neve, entitled *The Homecoming*, which moves me very much and which always puts me in mind of Cafavy's poem. In the foreground is a quayside and there, standing with their backs to us, are seven robed figures, looking out to sea. In the sky is an enormous moon reflected in the ocean below and in that reflected light we see a ship with sails approaching the harbour. Is it Theseus returning home after his many voyages, or is it each one of us returning home at the end of our lives?

There is no end to living for time flowers into eternity. At the moment of dying we do indeed run out of time, like an emptied hourglass, but it is at that moment, as from an endless spring, that we begin to fill to overflowing with eternity. There is a time for dying and there is a time for being born anew.

Postscript

And slowly answer'd Arthur from the barge:
'The old order changeth, yielding place to new,
And God fulfils himself in many ways,
Lest one good custom should corrupt the world
If thou should'st never see my face again,
Pray for my soul. More things are wrought by prayer
Than this world dreams of. Wherefore, let thy voice
Rise like a fountain for me night and day.
For what are men better than sheep or goats
That nourish a blind life within the brain,
If, knowing God, they lift not hands of prayer
Both for themselves and those who call them friend?
For so the whole round earth is every way
Bound by gold chains about the feet of God.

From Tennyson, *The Passing of Arthur*

Bibliography

Auster, Paul, *Moon Palace* (Faber, 1990)

Barks, Coleman, *Selected Poems of Rumi*

Bowra, Sir Maurice, *Primitive Song* (Weidenfeld and Nicolson, 1962)

Cafavy, translated by Rae Dalven, *Ithaca, The Complete Poems of C.P. Cavafy* (Hogarth Press, 1948)

Campbell, Joseph, with Moyers, Bill, *The Power of Myth* (Doubleday: New York, 1988)

Cary, Joyce, *To Be A Pilgrim*

Cervières, Sydney Keyes, *The Selected Poems* (Routledge and Kegan Paul, 1945)

Chesterton, G.K., *The Spirit of Christmas* (Xanadu, 1984)

Conradi, Peter, *Going Buddhist* (Short Books, 2004)

Conradi, Peter, *Calm-Abiding Meditation-Ox Herding* (an unpublished lecture)

Cox, Harvey, *Seduction of the Spirit* (Simon and Schuster, 1973)

Craig-Wild, Peter, *Tools for Transformation* (Darton Longman and Todd, 2002)

Déchanet, Pere, *Christian Yoga* (Burns and Oates, 1960)

Duras, Marguerite, translated by Barbara Bray, *The Lovers of Viorne* (Calder and Boyars, 1967)

Edinger, Ed. F., *The Christian Archetype* (Inner City Books: Toronto, 1987)

Fontana, David and Slack, Ingrid, *Teaching Meditation to Children* (Watkins, 2007)

Ford, Michael, *Report from the Shoreline* (Spirituality Dominican Publications)

Harvey, Andrew, *A Journey to Ladakh* (Jonathan Cape, 1983)

Hussein, Ed, *The Islamist*

Jamison, Dom Christopher, *Finding Sanctuary* (Weidenfeld and Nicolson, 2006)

Jaworski, Joseph, *Synchronicity: the inner path of leadership*, (Berrett-Koehler, 1998)

King, Ursula, *Towards A New Mysticism*

Kornfield, Jack, *After the Ecstasy the Laundry* (Rider, 2000)

Lanyado, Dr Monica, *Psycho-analytic Perspectives* (Dec 2008)